"*Happy Church* is a welcome reminder that [...] life and that the desire for happiness is not t[...] in thoroughly readable and wonderfully fu[...] [...] that the happy life is about wanting to be used for God's glory. This book is the ideal companion for anyone who wishes to bring the happiness of full surrender in Christ to their own life and their faith community."

D. Michael Lindsay, president, Gordon College

"*Happy Church* is not just a corrective to the dour, joyless expressions of Christian faith commonly found in American churches. It's actually a primer on the sturdy practices that have animated healthy churches for centuries. With clear, accessible prose, McConnell interweaves ancient insights from the early church fathers with contemporary scholarship and compelling illustrations from his own pastoral ministry. While I doubt the word 'happy' can be rescued from its often-shallow connotations, McConnell has achieved something better: he has resurrected the glorious doctrine of the church for a generation that has lost it. Christians seeking to enrich their experience of Christ in the local church will do well to read this book."

Walter Henegar, senior pastor, Atlanta Westside Presbyterian Church

"Pessimists, skeptics and curmudgeons take note: you are allowed to be happy—and so is your church! In a world where books about brokenness and suffering top the bestseller lists, *Happy Church* comes as a breath of fresh and joy-filled air. Using a captivating blend of biblical research, scholarly insight and real-life encounters with gladness, Tim McConnell's *Happy Church* gives us both reason and permission to rejoice, even in life's most difficult moments. Yes, life is hard (and the Bible says it will be so) but as Tim McConnell says, 'Your church is allowed to be happy!' And the good news, according to McConnell, is that the happiness is already in there—we just need to know how to get it out."

Jodie Berndt, author of *Praying the Scriptures for Your Children*

"Authentic Christianity is hugely attractive—it is also happy. The church in the West could learn much from our biblical ancestors—and also our brothers and sisters who worship in less hospitable conditions, yet display a deeply irrepressible vibrancy, life in all its fullness. This book argues the point and is rooted in practice. The biblical church is enthusiastic, passionate and energetic: a community of people whose encounter with God has made them genuinely happy. This book reflects Tim McConnell's authentic Christian faith and the happy attitude that characterizes his growing church. Authentic book, authentic pastor, authentic man."

Andrew Alden, vicar, St. Paul's Church, Weston-super-Mare, UK

"I am delighted and honored to recommend to you a wonderful resource titled *Happy Church*. My good friend Tim McConnell has done an outstanding job of capturing the essence of why the church should be the happiest place on earth. For any pastor or staff member attempting to instill a spirit of joy, this is a must-read!"

Dwight "Ike" Reighard, president and CEO, MUST Ministries, senior pastor, Piedmont Church

"I have known Tim since his days in college, and this book reflects his personality—a solid, biblical faith combined with the ability to stand back from the Christian religion and examine it in the context of following Jesus. This book challenges us to think not about what we do but why we do it as people who want to live lives reflecting Jesus and his love for us. This is a good resource that reminds all pastors to examine their first love."

Simon Barnes, chief executive officer, Send a Cow

"The need for happiness in Christ's church is not superficial or sentimental; rather, it is critical for those in the church and for its mission. It is about worship, being the family of God and love for neighbor."

Justin S. Holcomb, coauthor of *Rid of My Disgrace*

"Tim McConnell's *Happy Church* is a breath of fresh air. Here we have a wonderful, clear, grounded antidote for Eeyore Christians everywhere. *Happy Church* is a book the church needs in a serious way."

Don Everts, author of *Go and Do*

"Curmudgeons, beware! *Happy Church* wrests a smile from stress-addled doers and incites rampant hope in those grappling with suffering. Scripture provides the melody and McConnell calls forth voices from his merry band, including Lewis, Chesterton, Piper and Ortberg, irresistibly beckoning the reader into joy. This book is a delight."

Glenn Lucke, Docent Research Group

"In this highly individualistic culture, happiness can often be reduced to self-serving emotionalism. *Happy Church* is a timely book for those living in a society desperately seeking happiness through medication, therapy, sex, consumerism and false promises of prosperity. McConnell offers an important corrective that is theologically grounded in the Scriptures and draws from the rich history of Christian tradition."

Tony Tian-Ren Lin, research scholar, Institute for the Advanced Study in Culture, University of Virginia

"Church, get your happy on! *Happy Church* invites Christians to the 'serious business of happy' as God's beloved. Tim takes us to the well of Scripture and the great thinkers of the church to give us deep and practical tools for Christians to be the happy that God always intended—and the happy the world is longing to have."

Marnie Crumpler, executive pastor, Peachtree Presbyterian Church

Happy Church

Pursuing Radical Joy as the People of God

• • •

TIM McCONNELL

Foreword by JOHN ORTBERG

IVP Books

An imprint of InterVarsity Press
Downers Grove, Illinois

InterVarsity Press
P.O. Box 1400, Downers Grove, IL 60515-1426
ivpress.com
email@ivpress.com

InterVarsity Press® is the book-publishing division of InterVarsity Christian Fellowship/USA®, a movement of students and faculty active on campus at hundreds of universities, colleges and schools of nursing in the United States of America, and a member movement of the International Fellowship of Evangelical Students. For information about local and regional activities, visit intervarsity.org.

Scripture quotations, unless otherwise noted, are from The Holy Bible, English Standard Version, copyright © 2001 by Crossway Bibles, a division of Good News Publishers. Used by permission. All rights reserved.

While any stories in this book are true, some names and identifying information may have been changed to protect the privacy of individuals.

Cover design: David Fassett
Interior design: Beth McGill

ISBN 978-0-8308-4456-2 (print)
ISBN 978-0-8308-9369-0 (digital)

Printed in the United States of America ∞

Library of Congress Cataloging-in-Publication Data

McConnell, Tim, 1973-
  Happy church : pursuing radical joy as the people of God / Tim McConnell ; foreword by John Ortberg.
    pages cm
  Includes bibliographical references.
  ISBN 978-0-8308-4456-2 (pbk. : alk. paper)
  1. Happiness—Religious aspects—Christianity. 2. Church. 3. Christian life. I. Title.
BV4647.J68M38 2016
  253—dc23

                                                                              2015036061

P	21	20	19	18	17	16	15	14	13	12	11	10	9	8	7	6	5	4	3	2	1

Y	33	32	31	30	29	28	27	26	25	24	23	22	21	20	19	18	17	16

For Abigail,

my companion in joy.

Contents

Foreword

John Ortberg

• • •

If we were to look at the average Christian, and (reasonably) assume that we are trying to learn from God to be like God, we might assume that God is a relatively grumpy being. We are so grumpy ourselves that we would have to assume our God is miserable. Gandhi reportedly said, "I like your Christ, I do not like your Christians. Your Christians are so unlike your Christ." I like your Christ; I just don't like your Christians. Christians, what kind of Christ are we reflecting?

God is not a grumpy God. God created all things out of nothing by sheer love. God made everything good and beautiful just because he wanted it that way. God is a joy-loving and a joy-giving God.

Jonathan Edwards taught that God is happy. He said, "The whole of God's internal good or glory is in these three things, his infinite *knowledge*, his infinite virtue or *holiness*, and his infinite joy and *happiness*."[1] God is all-knowing, all-righteous—and all happy! He's not just omniscient and omnipresent and omnipotent, he's *omnicelebrant*. Our relationship with God is a gift. It is the gift God gives that we get to participate in these aspects, these attributes of God: knowledge, virtue and joy. We get to know God, we get to receive transforming power to be made holy like God over time, and we get to participate in God's joy—God's happiness. God communicates these aspects of himself to us in his glory, and we return them with praise.

One of the primary purposes of the church, one of the main reasons why God has placed a church on earth and gathered us up to be a part of it, is so the world can know who he is by looking at the people he redeems and gathers.

Do our gatherings reflect a fundamentally happy and joyful God? Can you taste and see that the Lord is good when you gather in Christian fellowship at your church? Does your church stand out in your community as a refuge of gladness, a bastion of joy, a reservoir of happiness? Are you participating in the joy of God?

The truth is, we who are leaders have a lot to say about the tone and culture of our church. And I'm not merely talking to pastors here but teachers and small group leaders, worship leaders, Bible study facilitators, youth group counselors, nursery workers, moms and dads and big brothers and little sisters and pew sitters and even the guy who just came because his friend forced him after he lost a bet on a round of golf. All of us. We all contribute. We all play a part to make the church the church. Is it a happy church? God is a joy-giving God.

I've not only read Tim's book but I get to work with him on a regular basis. He has spent a lot of time reading smart thinkers from periods of the history of the church I have only heard about in seminary! I love the way his brain works, and I'm so grateful for this resource he has put together for us to examine our life together as the body of Christ.

There is deep meaning to the things we do together as a church. These things all have deeper meaning, and just to remind ourselves of what we're doing when we gather, and we sing, and we pray, and we read Scripture, and we laugh, and we cry—just to sit back and think about the meaning of these is so refreshing. It's renewing. It's joy giving and hope filling.

Reading Tim's book changed the way I lead. I want to lead a happy people of God, and that means I want to lead with more joy, more happiness, more exuberance because of what Christ has done for us. It's important. It reflects a joyful God when the people of God celebrate joy.

Read it. And stop being such a grump.

Happy the people whose God is the LORD!

PSALM 144:15 RSV

Preface

• • •

Happy *church* is a risky term. Staid Christians have been trained not to use the word *happy* to describe the Christian faith— it's too flighty. And to the outsider or nonbeliever "happy church" sounds like an oxymoron. "Happy church? I've never seen one!"

God made the church to be a resource for joy, a repository of gladness and a manifestation of happiness rooted in heaven.

The church is countercultural from its inception. It did not emerge from the world in the natural course of history. It is not a product of human advances, like democracy or the technological revolution. The church does not owe its birth to the world, and its destiny does not depend on human progress. For this reason the community of faith we call the church always runs against the grain of the culture in which it sits. It is radically countercultural. Its goals are different from the world's goals, its values are different from the world's values, and its happiness is different from the world's happiness. The happy church is the people of God in pursuit of a radical joy, not dependent on this world and its ways.

I want to explore happiness in the church, not so much how to install it as how to recognize that it is already there. Your church is allowed to be happy. Read these chapters, take a look at your own church with new eyes, searching for the roots of happiness. Be reminded of the purposes of the community of faith and become more aware of what God is doing in your midst. Maybe God is already making your church happy, and you just didn't know it.

God intends to make his promises come true, to create pockets of happy people in this world—people whose joy serves his purposes for his glory.

My prayer is to see a generation of happy, joy-filled and joy-driven churches in our times. I want the joy of what the Lord has done for us to overflow in our hearts, in our families, in our churches and onto the streets of our cities.

We, the church, must be the culture of joy God has made us to be, and together we can cultivate a climate of happiness. The church is a community built on faith that God is good, that God is beautiful, that God is worthy of praise. And this God has given us life together as a gift. God has done great things for us; he has made us glad.

> Then our mouth was filled with laughter,
>   and our tongue with shouts of joy;
> then they said among the nations,
>   "The LORD has done great things for them."
> The LORD has done great things for us;
>   we are glad. (Psalm 126:2-3)

1

Getting Serious About Happiness

Everyone wants to be happy, to be blessed. . . .
God's ways and God's presence are where we
experience the happiness that lasts.

EUGENE PETERSON

• • •

He knelt down on the stage. Even in the kneeling you could see the awkwardness. He never really fit in at high school. His family was different. His clothes were different. He was different. But recently he had become the most effective evangelist that high school had seen in years.

And he was getting baptized.

All of us were holding back tears. It meant so much for us as a church to have a young man, eighteen years old, kneeling for baptism in our worship service. We had been praying God would use our church more effectively to reach the next generation.

Nobody would be posting "One baptism today" on Twitter in an attempt to keep up with the nearby megachurches posting their dozens. But for us this was a special morning.

Zack got up and the pastor gave him a minute to address the

church. "I was pretty lost, honestly. I didn't fit in. But I met a few guys who invited me to Young Life, and I wanted what they had. I gave my life to Christ. Then I came here and saw you guys had the same thing. You all just seemed so happy. I knew something was there, and I wanted it. I still want it, but now I can feel it in me too."

He was about to sit down and then thought to punctuate it: "Jesus is awesome!"

A People in Pursuit of Happiness

Is your church happy? Most of us are not sure how to answer that question. It seems like church should be a happy place, right?

Yes, it should. Church should be a happy place not because we want it to be but because God wants it to be. God has intentions and purposes for the church, and oddly enough, those purposes include instilling joy in his people.

The church's influence on the world depends on its joy.

Joy is available to any church of any size, and yet joy often sits by as a neglected resource for most churches. It is time to equip Christians to release joy in their churches, to live into a neglected aspect of the Christian life—we are meant to be a people in pursuit of radical joy.

The church's influence on the world depends on its joy.

The direct pursuit of happiness rarely produces happiness. But foundational reasons to be happy exist in every church—if it is truly the church. There are blessings unleashed in the common activities of every church. Large or small, in any context or any language, churches have a number of consistent patterns of behavior so simple they often go unnoticed. The tragedy comes when a church forgets why it does the things it does, when these behaviors become dead ritual and mindless habit. Happiness perishes in the arid climate of empty ceremonialism. When a church has lost touch with deep happiness and joy in Christ, it is time to reexamine these common activities we regularly share and uncover the blessings of God we find in them. In restoring this understanding, we just might restore the foundations for a community of pervasive celebration and gladness.

C. S. Lewis said, "Joy is the serious business of heaven."[1] *Happy* is serious business. I believe we need to learn the serious business of happiness in our Christian life together in the church. We need to learn to fight for joy in our churches.

It is not a superficial matter. Church in the Western world is declining. *Church* has developed such a bad reputation that some will be surprised I even choose to use the word. Many pastors avoid saying "church" at all—as impossible as that is—because too many people associate the word *church* with a bad experience, a time they visited a dark and musty building filled with little or no joy, where the people whispered and wept in dark shadows. Church has been starved of its happiness.

It's time to bring "happy" back.

A Thicker Happy

People get nervous about the word *happy*.

When I say "happy," I mean something deeper than simple emotion. The word is used more philosophically. Happiness can be viewed as a superficial emotional state coming as the product of *happenstance*—things *happen* to be right, and that *happens* to make me *happy*. Those words are related, deriving from the word *hap*, meaning "chance" or "good luck." But happiness can be more than that. It can also signify a deep longing and universal human search for fulfillment, blessing and meaning.

We are not chasing superficial, circumstantial happiness. There is thicker happiness than that, deeper happiness. We must pursue happiness at its depth, where it includes more than a favorable moment. This thicker meaning includes the sad kind of happiness, like when a loved one passes away but we know she is with Christ, or the tired kind of happiness after a hard day's work. There is a kind of happiness right in the middle of pain and struggle. I am talking about a thicker happy than the superficial sentimentality of the moment.

Some prefer to use the word *joy* to discuss this kind of happiness. In many ways I am using *happiness* and *joy* interchangeably or at least trying to restore them as partners. We are accustomed to stratifying happiness and joy these days. In sermon after sermon pastors say it's wrong to pursue happiness. The big problem, in their view, is that everybody wants to be happy, and they abandon all morals and constraint in pursuit of the momentary satisfaction of a thirst for happiness. Happiness and joy are cast as opposites to prove the point, making one superficial and the other profound. This works in the pulpit but is nonsense everywhere else.

In reference works *joy*, *happiness* and *gladness* are defined the same way. So what's the difference? I take *joy* and *gladness* to refer to something more internal, the feeling of being right with the world and settled in the confidence of our own well-being. Happiness is both the internal feeling and the exuberant expression of these qualities. Happiness starts within but is expressed without.

Happiness, gladness and joy are not opposing forces, and they certainly are not sitting on top of one another like layers of a cake. Joy goes all the way up and all the way down, and so does happiness. There can be superficial levels of joy and happiness, and there can be happiness and joy at the depths of our being. Joy and happiness go hand in hand.

We can talk about joy. We can talk about gladness. Why can't we talk about happiness too? I stand by the Bible's promises. The psalmist says we will be glad. Paul admonishes us to rejoice. Jesus told the crowd, "Happy are you. . . . Be happy and glad" (Matthew 5:11-12 GNT).

We are not fools to believe in and seek happiness. Yes, we know that life is hard. We don't expect every day to be a day at the fair now that we walk with Jesus. Jesus warned of great difficulty in this life. There will be suffering, but those who walk with Christ will feel differently about it, knowing that it is impermanent and passing, knowing that Jesus has overcome it all and we will share in his victory in due course. Even our suffering has a dimension of happiness to it that it would not have without Jesus.

Pastor John Ortberg writes, "The salvation of your soul is not just about where you go when you die. The word *salvation* means healing or deliverance at the deepest level of who we are in the care of God through the presence of Jesus. Sooner or later, your world will fall apart. What will matter then is the soul you have constructed."[2] Life is full of horrible tragedies. The world is filled with brokenness and pain. Churches promising constant situational happiness are floating a false dream and distorting the purposes of Jesus. But salvation means "the soul you have constructed" rests on something more solid than your current circumstances. This resting place is grounds for gladness, solid grounds for both feeling and expressing joy. The Bible calls this "happiness."

There are those who peddle situational happiness, promising immediate and superficial rewards for the right performance of religious or spiritual duties. Happiness is much too serious business for me to fall in with that crowd. There will be hardships, there will be trials, there will be tears and there is no way to avoid them. Nobody should promise us otherwise. But in them all, if we are with Christ there is nevertheless a promise that we will be happy even in the trials.

True happiness is not built on situational foundations. Any who have had the privilege to travel on missions know this. My wife, Abigail, and I have led five short-term mission trips to Kenya over the last dozen years, and we love to be there ourselves. But more than that we love to share the experience with others. It's amazing what that experience can do to shape a Christian disciple. One thing we hear time and again from people we bring to Kenya is: "I just can't believe how happy the people are! I can't believe the strength of their faith, and I can't believe their profound happiness."

The surprise stems from their deep-seated assumptions of the source of happiness. The kids in the communities we serve there have nothing by way of possessions. No luxuries, not even all their basic needs. Their futures are uncertain and carry little promise of success, as the average American conceives of success. But they know the Lord in deep and rich ways. When we fly to Africa from the suburbs and observe these kids, we have a rotten tendency to think they have no business being happy. But they are. They are deeply, profoundly happy in the Lord. They live out a rich faith in Jesus Christ surrounded by a community of joy providing love and encouragement, hope and laughter. They live out a thicker happiness than the materialistic American consumer will ever know.

We can be happy—foundationally happy, deep in our core—if our happiness is rooted in the right source. Tears may come, and waves of emotion may wrack our spirit, but we will remember a deep foundation of joy and carry the hope that our strength in happiness will return. So we remain calm and settled even as the tears well up. This is the thicker happiness we seek.

Happy or Blessed

"Shouldn't we use the word *blessed* instead?" some may ask. Our most common English translations of the Bible too often use *blessed* when the actual word in Hebrew or in Greek means "happy."

Happy and *blessed* are two different things. One is a comment on what we are receiving from the outside: blessing. The other is a claim on the very status of our soul: happy.

A person does feel happy when blessed, but that doesn't mean we should say "blessed" when we mean "happy." God promises the internal state of our soul will be different because of his blessing. Because of what God does for us, the soul will be filled with joy and express happiness. *Blessing produces happiness.*

In the Old Testament the word we're looking for is *asher*. It first appears in Genesis, when Leah is overjoyed at the birth of a son for Jacob (through her servant Zilpah as a surrogate): "And Leah said, 'Happy am I! For women have called me happy.' So she called his name Asher [Happy]" (Genesis 30:13).

The word is used repeatedly to describe those who love the Lord, fear the Lord, serve the Lord, taste the Lord and see that he is good, and who simply belong to the Lord and know that he is their God. It brackets a well-known Proverb about finding wisdom (Proverbs 3:13-18), used as the first and last words of that passage.

This word, *asher*, is so important it appears as the very first word of the book of Psalms. One scholar identifies no less than thirty-four "happiness psalms" based on *asher* and its synonyms.[3] Almost all of them are translated to the English word *blessed* and its cognates. The bottom line is, when we read the word *blessed* in the Psalms and much of the Old Testament, we should hear the word *happy* in the back of our mind. It is probably *asher*.

The same thing is true in the New Testament translations with the Greek word *makarios*. *Makarios* is most directly translated as "happy," but most translators use *blessed*. Perhaps because Jesus used the word in the Sermon on the Mount, our translators just can't stomach writing "Happy are the sad." As New Testament scholar Frederick Dale Bruner writes, "Is it good news to tell the poor and miserable that they are, in fact, happy?"[4] He supposes not, but that is what Jesus said!

There is a type of happiness in God that trumps sadness, even in the midst of it. In James we read: "The one who looks into the perfect law, the law of liberty, and perseveres, being no hearer who forgets but a doer who acts, he will be *blessed* in his doing" (James 1:25, emphasis added). Doesn't that give the impression that if we do the right things, God will respond by releasing blessing? It promotes a works-righteousness mentality. But the word is *makarios* (happy). James is saying that "you will be *happy* in your doing." Your soul will be happy living in the liberty of the designs of God outlined for you in God's law—happy *as you do these things*. The Bible says more about being happy than we realize.

We could use the word *blessed* and escape some risk of misunderstanding, but what are we losing of God's promises? I want to hold on to the claim of happiness. The state of our soul is meant to be different because we walk with God. The state of our soul is categorically altered because we are in Christ.

There is a truth here often missed, tragically overlooked and mysteriously neglected, that the Christian life is indeed a happy life.

The Happy-Go-Lucky Pastor

An early reader of this manuscript said, "I want to know more about Tim. Is this guy just naturally happy all the time, or what?" When my wife read that, she laughed out loud. Embarrassingly loud. I mean it startled the kids. Then she looked up at me sheepishly and said with pity, "Oh, Honey!"

She knows me better.

We dated in college before she came to Christ, and one day we were talking about faith. She said, "Faith for me is a form of positive thinking. I know everything will work out in the end. That's faith." I cut into her, "What? Things don't just work out. Most people in the world live lives of quiet desperation marked with failure and disappointment, punctuated in the end by tragedy and death." She was charmed.

Just after we were married, we each pulled out books to read on the beach. My wife patiently but firmly explained I would not be reading Søren Kierkegaard's *The Sickness unto Death* on our honeymoon. When Abigail and I met, she was the optimist and I was the pessimist—but I was the one who knew the Lord. I was sour, and I was the one saved by Christ. What was wrong with this picture?

Thank God, Abigail committed her life to Christ despite the pictures I had painted. She came to Christ in joy and continued in his joy to become a faithful and mature believer, fully devoted to her Lord and Savior in every way and modeling that faith to all around her. Her trust moved from faith in *faith* to faith in Jesus Christ, the only one who can save us from this world of sin.

But it was no thanks to my nasty moods.

I was a cynical and sad young man for many years. My parents' divorce, although as friendly as a divorce can be, had left some scars. I kept to myself as a kid.

But I had been blessed by people bent on joy in the Lord. In Young Life it is a crime to bore a kid with the gospel. It's "illegal" to tell someone what Jesus has done to save his or her soul and not celebrate it with some measure of happiness. I was a Young Life kid. They pushed me to slip down the monster waterslide. They prodded me to release my inhibitions and play silly games, laugh at goofy skits and sing songs I had never heard. All of it opened my heart to receive the Lord I had somehow known and still ignored all my childhood.

This ministry of joy made all the difference in the world to me. I decided I wanted to do the same for others, so I studied how they did it. Celebration was involved, and it wasn't accidental or superficial. It was celebration for a purpose.

It took me a long time to take happiness seriously as a Christian. We are the right, the correct, not the happy. We suffer and are martyred; we don't smile and laugh. As I was doing my doctoral work I read the accounts of martyrs and wondered why they smiled and sang and looked like angels when they died. Is there such a thing as a happy martyr? Actually, in first-century Christianity there is no other kind.

Reading Augustine, I wondered what he meant by happiness. Here was a man at least as tyrannized by his sins as I was and at least as cynical about the world—but he spoke of happiness. Is happiness seriously a goal for a Christian?

I preached and taught for years, regularly returning to the theme: "The joy of the LORD is your strength" (Nehemiah 8:10); "Happy the people whose God is the LORD" (Psalm 144:15 RSV); "Rejoice in the Lord always; again I say, rejoice" (Philippians 4:4). Though we are realistic about this world, we are called to celebrate and walk in joy.

Is it okay to say that?

I wondered if I was turning into some kind of health-and-wealth preacher. Those who preach faith as a pretext for leveraging God into the service of their own gratuitous gain have stepped over the line. But I wasn't preaching anything like that. I was preaching the shining face of Stephen as he was stoned, the beatific joy in Polycarp as he was burned at the stake in the Roman Coliseum, and Jesus as he forgave and made plans for the future from the cross. It seems that Christians are most in touch with joy at the lowest points of suffering.

Something about happiness is profoundly world-overcoming. Something about happiness in Christ is victorious for his kingdom. It pokes the devil in the eye. It destroys strongholds of darkness, releases prisoners and lets the poor hear good news. Something about happiness strikes a blow.

Something about happiness is profoundly world-overcoming.

I like that. "In the world you have tribulation; but be of good cheer, I have overcome the world" (John 16:33 RSV).

Soon I found I was not alone. Jonathan Edwards believed in the happiness of God and taught the importance of our share in it. Richard Foster closes his book on spiritual disciplines with a chapter titled "The Discipline of Celebration." Oh yeah, the whole book is titled *Celebration of Discipline*. How did I miss that? John Ortberg seems in touch with happiness. His chapter "A Dee-Dah Day" in *The Life You've Always Wanted* opens up dimensions of glee in God I knew were there but had never articulated. John Piper argues vehemently for joy in the face of dour critics. Yes, to walk with Christ is better than to walk without him. Go ahead and say it. Actually it's part of the gospel message.

No, I am not naturally happy. I embrace the practice of happiness.

It isn't as though Jesus has kept this happiness hidden. It is part of almost every story he told! "These things I have spoken to you, that my joy may be in you, and that your joy may be full," Jesus said to his disciples in John 15:11. Not only that "my joy" might be instilled in you but that "your joy" might be full. Those are different joys. God's joy and our joy. Parable after parable reveals Jesus' investment in joy.

God is invested in our joy. An honest response to that—an intellectually and spiritually honest response—is to be happy.

Maybe we should take that seriously.

2

Where Is the Happy Church?

The greatest gift the church can give society is a glimpse,
however fleeting, of another city, where the angels
keep "eternal festival" before the face of God.

Robert Louis Wilken

● ● ●

"We just watch sermons online."

"What?"

This was a problem. One of my key leaders in Law Christian Fellowship at the Virginia School of Law and his newlywed wife had apparently given up on church. I knew it was a problem, but suddenly I didn't know how to say *why* it was a problem.

"You don't go to church?"

"We got sick of looking around. And we're only here for a couple of years, so we decided to just watch sermons online."

"But you need community. You need fellowship. You need to be around people who aren't like you, younger and older and diverse." He still seemed unconvinced. "Plus, there are donuts."

Christianity is a community activity. It's a team sport, not a solo engagement. It's full contact.

We are a *people* in pursuit of radical joy. We can't do it alone.

God has done great things for the church, wonderful things. The church is the bride of Christ; he has fought to redeem the church. It receives promise after promise, blessing after blessing from God. The punishment the church deserves for disobedience has been taken away by Jesus, and the people of God are free to walk into heaven and eternal life simply by faith in him. Jesus died for the church and paid the penalty once and for all on the cross. The church is a rescued people; it ought to be a community marked by gladness and gratitude. We have to be present to be a part of that.

At its core, Christian fellowship is joy in communion with Christ. That means the closer we get to the core of the church, the more powerfully we should feel joy. Jesus has brought us into a relationship with him. He has created the communion, knitting us together with him at the very core. That makes us happy. It's like a tuning fork whose sound waves, once touched off, resonate through our community, setting the tone and drawing us toward itself.

But we have to be there to feel that.

Sure, there are disagreements and periods in the life of the church marked with sadness. The life of a church is like any other, filled with highs and lows. But whether up or down we are warmed by the light of Christ, and we cultivate and defend a culture of happiness and joy.

The church claims the cross as its defining symbol. We meet under the cross to proclaim the most significant saving act of all time. We wear crosses around our necks and on our shirts, and we stick them on our cars. Some of us tattoo the cross on our arms. We use the cross to proclaim what Christ has done for us.

But to the world a smile may say more.

There's a reason God wants his people to be happy.

A Gathering Like No Other

The church is God's alternative community gathered on earth. It is where Christians live an alternative life, escaping the tyrannical bounds of a determined existence to find open possibilities we never dreamed. Different rules apply here. Racial and social divisions dissolve to make a new way of life available. Friendships and partnerships emerge that are impossible in the ordinary economies of life and culture. This has been true from the very beginning; the dividing lines disappeared and Christians said, "Here there is not Greek and Jew, . . . barbarian, Scythian, slave, free; but Christ is all, and in all" (Colossians 3:11).

The early church was such a diverse gathering of people from all walks of life that the Roman authorities could not figure out why they were getting together. What is this? Some kind of political movement? A funeral society? A social club? What brings slaves and masters, women and men, rich and poor together to meet like this? They couldn't figure it out, and it gave them great anxiety.

Yes, the picture I am painting is ideal. But even if there is some distance between that vision and the reality we meet on Sunday morning, the ideal is still there—in church.

Church is grounds for a new way of being together.

As beautiful as that is, it's only the beginning of the magic we find in these communities. Churches are sacred temples of men and women constructed with God himself as designer and architect. In the world churches stand distinct, beckoning us to the city of God and whispering of rebellion against the present order. When we are there, our minds expand like Jacob's and we glimpse ladders of angels ascending and descending between earth and heaven. Church opens a window to a world bigger and fuller than the one we have known. A different way of life is here. God is here. "How awesome is this place!" (Genesis 28:17).

Church opens a window to a world bigger and fuller than the one we have known. A different way of life is here.

Sometimes on a long drive I watch steeples and churches go by and imagine the praise rising up from each holy site like smoke from a hundred small campfires. From each fire the smoke rises like a pillar until it joins and collects in a great swarming cloud filling the sky and diffusing into the heavens. Isn't this the view from above? Each holy gathering lifts worship and praise; up it rises to converge until the praise of all the world pours into the throne room of grace. How beautiful!

At the base of each pillar of praise, gathered around each fire is a community of faith. They are the lucky ones. Circled together, they warm themselves by the fire, and their faces glow in its light. God has gathered each of these circles, each alternative community, and placed them just where they sit. It is no accident. Some are large and rambunctious groups, and others are small and quiet circles, but large or small, each has its own true fire burning.

God has arranged each one so that in every place the lost can see the fire—or at least smell the aroma or hear the glad songs of the alternative community of Jesus Christ—and be drawn toward Jesus' warmth and light.

This is God's plan, not ours. It is how Jesus Christ is still at work in this world to seek and to save the lost. This is the happy church.

Joy is the untapped resource of the church today. Simple joy. Abiding gladness. The happy songs and warm coffee clutched around the fires of genuine praise. Joy is equally available to churches large and small. It requires no wealth or status but is enjoyed by the church of any size or stature just the same. It requires no program, no staffing, no subscription service or consultation. It's available right now.

Joy, like honey, tastes the same whether we are a king or a pauper. Whether slathered across a scone on the back of a yacht in the Mediterranean or squeezed out of a packet onto a biscuit at the bottom of a West Virginia coal mine, when it hits the tongue it's just as sweet. That's joy.

Has your church lost its taste for joy and gladness?

What if every church in every city became a happy alternative community known for the experience of joy, and the moment an outsider approached the fires of praise they felt immersed in gladness? What if when they left they tasted the sweetness of true joy on their lips?

This is the happy church. It is something worth pursuing.

Locating a Happy Church

Where on earth is the happy church? It may be closer than you think. We may be tempted to run from our own struggling churches in search of an alternative community so happy it stands out in a world of discontent. (They are out there!) But I believe most of us need to commit to creating and restoring the happy people of God right where we are. Many churches have lost their genuine happiness in Christ, and joy remains an *untapped* resource. But each church already has what it needs to be happy.

It's up to us to find the happiness again. But how?

God has already installed the joy. The gladness is already present. God has already given the church everything it needs to be faithful to Christ.

There is great power to the word *why*. *Why* is very motivating. *Why* is about purpose, intent and deeper meaning. People can suffer through just about anything so long as they know why. And people celebrate when they know why they are doing the normal activities of church life.

As Simon Sinek points out, Martin Luther King Jr. is not famous for his "I Have a Plan" speech. It was "I Have a Dream." A dream is a vision for the future, a purpose and a destination. It grants meaning.[1]

Much joy and happiness is unleashed when a community knows why it is doing what it is doing. Churches can learn from that. One of the quickest and easiest ways to tap into the untapped joy of the community of faith is to remind one another *why* we do the things we do.

Billy Graham said, "Christians are to rejoice. To do that, you need only to think of the great things God has done for you."[2] He doesn't make it sound like a suggestion, does he? First Thessalonians 5:16 commands that we "Rejoice always." The authors of the Westminster Catechism taught that "cheerfulness of spirit" is a duty connected to the sixth commandment, "Thou shalt not kill."[3] They must have thought cheerfulness is serious business to suggest that its opposite is murder. Happiness in the Christian community is serious business. We must take happiness in the church as a command from God, a worthy goal for every gathered church.

Yes, we are commanded to be the happy church, the happy people of God. It is our duty to rejoice, for God has done great things for us. But is it possible to command happiness? Is it fair to press a mood on one another as a duty? We are not able to force our emotions directly. Nothing can be more disconcerting than being told to be happy when we simply aren't. The most emotionally vulnerable among us may be easily pushed over the brink of despair.

C. S. Lewis wrote to his friend Sheldon Vanauken, "It is a Christian duty, as you know, for everyone to be as happy as he can."[4] A Christian duty! That makes it sound like we are to pull up our emotions from the bootstraps. But the same C. S. Lewis also wrote, "An obligation to feel can freeze feelings."[5] We could as easily make the sun rise as force ourselves into happiness.

Happiness cannot be forced. But what if our moods are the products of our attentions and activities?

We feel what we feel because we think what we think, and we actually do have the ability to choose the content of our thoughts.

We feel what we feel because we do what we do, and we have the ability to choose our actions.

"Be transformed by the renewal of your mind," writes Paul (Romans 12:2). This may be the place to start. We can actively select the focus of our attentions and direction of our thought life, and our moods and emotions will (for the most part) follow along behind. In that case, *then* do we have a duty?

There may also be a few intentional activities. Paul also says, "Present your bodies as a living sacrifice, holy and acceptable to God, which is your spiritual worship" (Romans 12:1). Eugene Peterson teaches, "We can *act* ourselves into a new way of feeling much quicker than we can *feel* ourselves into a new way of acting."[6]

Along with knowing the meaning behind the common activities of the church, there is a sacrificial commitment to participating in the common activities of the church. I'm going to worship. I'm going to sing. I'm going to attend that dinner, study the chosen passage of Scripture, and laugh at that tired and not-so-funny joke the pastor has already used five times in his sermons (please!). I'm committed to acting out the happiness of the community when I cannot say I naturally feel it. Isn't our choice of activity a duty?

Pushing the emotion of happiness in our churches may be as futile as pushing a string, but connect that string to the right thoughts and activities, and who knows . . . it may just straighten out.

So, rather than looking for a happy church, be ready to cultivate a happy church right where you are. The tools are at hand.

We need to start discussions about the foundations and reasons for deep happiness. As Billy Graham reminds us, we "need only to think." We need only to recount the wonderful things God has done for us. Like the words of Psalm 126:3, we need to repeat, "The LORD has done great things for us; we are glad."

The church is the congregation of believers redeemed by Jesus Christ. We were called out of darkness into everlasting light; we have heard the gospel of salvation, put our faith in Jesus Christ and so have received the Holy Spirit as a seal and guarantee. The church is that people for whom the wrath of God has become the love of God. Speaking of the church, the Bible says that while we were still enemies of God, Christ died for us. When we deserved nothing but eternal damnation by the hand of God because we were among those who rebelled against God's law and reign, God showed his love for us by sending his Son, Jesus Christ. We are the people for whom there is now "no condemnation," but we are made righteous by simply putting our faith in Jesus Christ and what he has done for us. The church is promised an eternal inheritance, guarded by the hand of God in heaven, where nothing can destroy it. Eternal life is our inheritance. The church is that group of people.

The church is the only group of people in the world who will not suffer the eternal consequences of our own sins and errors. Those consequences have been paid by Another, and we get the free gift of eternal life instead of the death wages of sin. The people of the church have the Word of God to guide us and light our path. We don't stumble in darkness but walk in the light of God in all our ways. We bear fruit in season, our leaf does not wither, but in all we do we prosper![7]

And all this is only the beginning of the remarkable promises of God for his people. Are these promises true or not? If not, fine. But if so, well, there is one word to describe the people for whom even one of those promises proves true: *happy.*

> Then our mouth was filled with laughter,
> and our tongue with shouts of joy,
> then they said among the nations,
> "The LORD has done great things for them." (Psalm 126:2)

Even the *nations* have something to say when they see the church receive the blessings of God; outsiders peer in and are amazed. The true church relishes what God has done and revels in his promises. The true church is happy.

When the world looks at the church and sees miserable people, all the promises of the gospel sound hollow. But what if your town looked at you and your church and saw a genuinely happy people?

God wants the world to see his happy people. If the church worships God and is happy, then the world looks on the church and wonders, *What makes them so happy?* That's what God intends. The promises and mighty acts of God are meant to produce a people who represent the goodness of God, a people washed in his grace and mercy who are passionate about his glory.

We All Thirst for Happiness

The people around us are ready to pursue happiness. It's who we are. The church must have a ready answer. The happy people of God must know the satisfying solution to the human thirst for happiness.

"All men seek happiness," Blaise Pascal wrote. "This is without exception. Whatever different means they employ, they all tend to this end. . . . This is the motive of every man."[8]

The desire to be happy is the secret and underlying motive of nearly every decision we make in our lives. I am not arguing for the morality or nobility or propriety of the pursuit of happiness. I am not arguing that pursuing happiness is right or virtuous. The pursuit of happiness simply is *the way it is.* This is the nature of humanity; we seek happiness. This is our very nature.

> **The desire to be happy is the secret and underlying motive of nearly every decision we make in our lives.**

Aristotle said, "We consider happiness the most desirable of all things."[9] We desire other things because we hope they will make us happy, but happiness we desire for its own sake. God built us with these longings for happiness. This is not a product of the fall;

it is not a product of sinfulness. God wired us to pursue happiness. Like water seeking its own level or air filling a vacuum, our souls run toward happiness.

Augustine's famous line in the opening of *Confessions* says a little bit about this: "[Lord,] you stir us so that praising you may bring us joy, because you have made us and drawn us to yourself, and our heart is unquiet until it rests in you."[10]

Augustine means that we are made with certain longings and desires that lead us toward God and leave us unsatisfied until we are at home in him. He talks about all the innate qualities he had as a boy, even though he was not yet a Christian. He had a desire for self-preservation, somehow knowing that life is better than death, existence than nonexistence. He hated being deceived and loved being right—"I delighted in truth." He enjoyed the comforts of friendship, "shrank from pain, groveling and ignorance." All these things, Augustine says, "are gifts from my God. I did not endow myself with them, but they are good, and together they make me what I am." These things were innate even before he was a Christian, and they made him want certain things—good things. The problem, he said, was not in the desire itself but in how he was seeking to satisfy it:

> But my sin was this, that I looked for pleasure, beauty, and truth not in him but in myself and his other creatures, and the search led me instead to pain, confusion, and error. My God, in whom is my delight, my glory, and my trust, I thank you for your gifts and beg you to preserve and keep them for me. Keep me, too.[11]

Augustine had innate desires to be fulfilled, correct and knowledgeable—he had innate desires to be happy. These desires were there long before he knew Christ. The sin was not the desires but the things he pursued to satisfy them instead of pursuing God.

God built us with desires for happiness and fulfillment. It's our nature to want to be happy. Like our desire for eternity and everlasting life—"he has put eternity into man's heart" (Ecclesiastes 3:11)—we have an innate desire for happiness, and Augustine found that this desire only came home in Jesus. The unquiet spirit continued in him until his soul rested in his Savior.

It is inherent in every human being to want this happiness and peace.

Of course people want to be happy. Of course they are pursuing happiness. It's at the very core of every decision they make. And we are not that different for being Christians. The desire for happiness is not sinful in itself. Sin points us in the wrong directions as we pursue happiness. Sin distorts our desire for happiness and bends it into a hopeless chase for immediate self-gratification. But the desire for happiness is not a sin, and seeking happiness is just part of who we are.

To fail to admit that is only foolishness, and it hurts our witness in the world. The pursuit of happiness is not wrong; the wrong pursuit of happiness—chasing after foolish things—is.

When it comes to happiness, Christians should not give up the pursuit but stand in contrast to the world by passionately pursuing happiness where it may actually be found. Finding happiness in Christ, we must be ready to present the solution to the world. Looking for happiness? It's right here!

Why hide the simple truth that we believe happiness is found in a life lived for Jesus? Philosopher Dallas Willard writes, "Jesus does not deny us personal fulfillment, but shows us the only true way to it. In him we 'find our life.'" So, then, the self-denial of the Christian life "is always the surrender of a lesser, dying self for a greater eternal one—the person God intended in creating you. Confidence in this is the occasion of 'greatly rejoicing, with joy unspeakable and full of glory' (1 Peter 1:8)."[12]

The church is a people aware of the unspeakable joy found on the other side of self-denial and commitment to Christ. The world searches and searches for happiness and is disappointed at every turn. When lost souls, so hungry for joy they hardly believe it even exists, show up on the doorstep of your church, what will they find?

The Art of Happiness

Princeton seminary professor Ellen Charry wrote *God and the Art of Happiness*, in which she argues that we have lost track of a long strand of Christian pursuit of happiness. In the early church, pursuit of happiness was a regular discussion and a noble pursuit. Like every other philosophy on the world stage, followers of Jesus believed they were on a way to a fulfilled and happy life in following Christ. In fact, they were certain of a happiness so strong, so enduring, that the sacrifices and pains they took to follow Jesus seemed like fleeting distractions compared to the eternal weight of glory they could already taste in Christ. In her book, professor Charry says Christianity lost this emphasis as Christians got more interested in self-sacrifice and self-denial—ironically, after the period of persecution was over.

All Christians wrestle with this question eventually: Are we living or dying? Isn't following Jesus about dying to myself? Paul wrote, "I have been crucified with Christ. It is no longer I who live" (Galatians 2:20). Yes, following Christ is about surrendering our lives to him. Dying to self. Insisting we allow everything in our lives to be taken up by him in sacrifice.

Then Paul says, "the life I now live . . ." *What? I thought you died!* But he says, "It is no longer I who live, but Christ who lives in me. And *the life I now live* in the flesh I live by faith in the Son of God, who loved me and gave himself for me" (Galatians 2:20). After the crucifixion, after dying to self, there is new life. Life from Christ wells up, and now there is a life in the flesh lived by faith founded on the love of God. That life is so strong that there is no experience, no pain, no suffering on earth that can dislodge it from the root of joy. That's why Paul says he can suffer through anything for Jesus. His life belongs to God.

What are we striving after as Christians? Are we striving after life or death? Life, of course! Even if we must pass through death—the death of the self—to get there. The end is joy in God, not misery.

The early pursuit of happiness got off-track. The Christian pursuit of the best in life gave way to a secular hedonism and self-ishness. As a religion, Christianity changed in the fourth century from being a beleaguered and victimized minority to an accepted and celebrated majority. Christianity was practiced at the highest levels, even by the emperor himself. This was a major change.

As time went on, Christians began to enjoy the comforts of worldly prestige and success. Happiness was once found in Jesus through the course of suffering and martyrdom, but now a super-ficial facsimile of happiness was easily available through wine and song and leisure. Wealth and success offered happiness at their fingertips. People pursued thin happiness in tenuous ways, and so they became selfish and never fully satisfied. To correct this, some Christians embraced harsh patterns of self-flagellation or other damaging ascetic practices. Monastic leaders would boast of how they abused their bodies through these practices, and when they died of malnutrition or other ailments from a life of intentional neglect of the body, their followers celebrated their austerity. The follower of Christ must not be selfish.

We are not supposed to be selfish, but we are still meant to pursue happiness over self-destruction! We are meant to be in-vested in finding the root of joy. There is a difference between un-healthy selfishness and appropriate love of self. There is such a thing as proper self-care, recognizing that God has given us a re-sponsibility to care for ourselves lovingly. We are embarrassed to say we are seeking happiness and health in following Jesus. But of course we are. There is good reason to be happy! There is a foundation for joy. There are ways we are meant to be connected to the taproot of joy, and there are ways this connection is meant to produce happiness.

Surveying Christian thought from the fourth century to the present, professor Charry points out the greatest Christian thinkers say true happiness is found in knowing God and being used for his purposes.

> Salvation is an excellent pattern of living that is personally rewarding because it advances God's intention for creation. . . . For Christians, happiness is being healed by Jesus with and for the wisdom of love. The church equips people to pursue eternal life that God may celebrate the work of his hands.[13]

The joy of the Lord is our strength. God is happy when we answer him and follow him and are rescued by him, therefore allowing ourselves to be healed enough to be used by him in the work of love. Then God celebrates, and we feel his joy. And we too are happy.

The people we go to church with know this already. They want this already. They long for deeper foundations of joy and more substantial expressions of happiness. We don't need to go far to find the happy church, we need to unleash the one we already know.

Uncovering the Treasure Already There

Jesus told parables about finding treasure of great value. In Matthew 13, for example, he teaches, "The kingdom of heaven is like treasure hidden in a field, which a man found and covered up. Then in his joy he goes and sells all that he has and buys that field" (Matthew 13:44).

Author and pastor John Piper found in this simple parable the truth of the gospel that has shaped his ministry for thirty years.

We might think it is a horrible thing to sacrifice all we have for Jesus. We might think this is what Christianity is: to give away what we want for something nobler, to sacrifice ourself and our happiness because that's what God demands of us. Piper thought that way as a young Christian. He thought he had to grit his teeth and commit to a life of misery because God demanded it. That, just like the man in the parable, we have to sell all we have for Jesus; we have to gather up everything we care about and get rid of it. Maybe this is the necessary misery of the Christian life, required for hell-avoidance.

But that theory did not account for three little words in this parable: *in his joy*.

Piper could not understand it. Why does it say the man did it with joy? We could understand doing it out of obligation: "in his duty." But the man doesn't glumly, sadly and sacrificially sell all he has for God to prove his worthiness for the kingdom. That's not what it says. *In joy* he sells all he has.

Why? Because, he has found the truth of the gospel and knows it's worth everything. When we have found the true joy that overcomes the world, we have found the promises of God not only for our eternal salvation but for the fullness of life right now. The man in the parable sells all he has *in joy* because he knows—he has faith—that the exchange is a good one. The treasure is of more value than anything he has. It is a treasure worth everything.

> **When we have found the true joy that overcomes the world, we have found the promises of God not only for our eternal salvation but for the fullness of life right now.**

This changed John Piper's life, his ministry and the lives of countless people he has taught. The Christian life is not an invitation to misery. It is grounded in joy. It is purposed in joy. It is driven by joy. It is a fullness of joy. It is a happy, happy life that begins now and stretches into eternity.

So where is the happy church? It is hidden right in front of our eyes. Just like the little phrase *in his joy* was hidden in broad daylight before John Piper. Where is the happy church? Right under the surface of the community we already know and love.

Piper says, "The happiest people in the world are the people who experience the mystery of 'Christ in them, the hope of glory' (Colossians 1:27)."[14] The church must fix its collective mind, its culture and the tone of every gathering and act on the ultimate joy of God. The happiest people in the world—that's us.

Does God want us happy? God is *for us*, not against us. God wants us eternally happy. God opens up avenues for our happiness. God has fought, is fighting and will fight to bring us to the fulfillment of all joy, happiness, peace and rest.

God has beaten the path of happiness down from where he is to where we are. And now it is our duty to walk that path back toward God with resolve. "For our aim must always be to reach that state of happiness in which no trouble shall distress us, and no error mislead us," wrote Augustine.[15]

Here is a foundation for happiness in our churches. God has called us together to be his people and to instruct us in the way of life everlasting. God is himself good and pure and holy. God is not malicious or angry or bitter. The wrath in God is wrath against evil because evil will rob us of true and eternal life. God, by nature, has determined to be in a posture of love and grace toward us, proven at the zenith by the death of his own Son, Jesus Christ, on the cross on our behalf. We can be constitutionally joyful, truly and deeply happy, because a good and happy God has made of us a people of his own.

Now, let's see what we get to do together.

Satisfied in the Word

When your words came, I ate them;
they were my joy and my heart's delight.

JEREMIAH 15:16 (NIV)

• • •

The church feeds on the Word of God. When the Word comes we consume it, and it becomes our joy. My church is part of a tradition that centers worship around Bible reading. We prepare for the Word, we receive the Word, we interpret the Word, then we move out under the Word into the world. Some think that type of church is sermon-centered, but it's not. It's Word-centered. The sermon is simply another way the church feeds together on the Word of God. As I teach in our new members classes, "You would have to be an absolute idiot to stand up right after the divine Word of God has been read, open your mouth and say something. Guess what that makes me?" A fool for the gospel, I guess.

Reading the Bible is the apex of the worship service.

The first picture of church is in Acts 2:42, "They devoted themselves to the apostles' teaching and the fellowship, to the breaking of bread and the prayers." The apostles' teaching is the Scriptures.

One of the earliest accounts of Christian worship after the Bible comes from Justin Martyr defending Christianity from public criticism to Roman authorities around AD 155. He wrote,

> And on the day called Sunday all who live in cities or in the country gather together in one place, and the memoirs of the Apostles or the writings of the prophets are read, as long as time permits. Then when the reader is finished, the Ruler in a discourse instructs and exhorts to the imitation of these good things. Then we all stand up together and offer prayers.[1]

We read the Scriptures. We read them every time we gather. In fact, if we haven't read them and received them in some way, we cannot call that gathering worship.

We are accustomed to feeding on the Word as part of worship. A church's relationship with the Scriptures may define its happiness. Nothing will erode the joy of the people of God more rapidly than separation from the Word, which feeds and nourishes us.

Like Jeremiah, when the Word comes we consume it—and it makes us glad (Jeremiah 15:16). This is Jeremiah speaking, the prophet of tears, the author of Lamentations. Jeremiah knew sadness and he knew joy. The Word of God fed him with joy, to his heart's delight. Perhaps like nothing else, the Word of God made Jeremiah happy.

> **Nothing will erode the joy of the people of God more rapidly than separation from the Word, which feeds and nourishes us.**

The Bible is a gift to the church. It is an honor to receive it. The fact that God wants us to have his Word and understand it is itself grounds for celebration. By feeding on the Word of God the church is nourished and sustained, transformed and empowered, and it is given a message and a mission to the world.

Martin Luther wrote,

> One thing, and only one thing, is necessary for the Christian
> life, righteousness, and freedom. That one thing is the most
> holy Word of God, the gospel of Christ. . . . The soul can do
> without anything except the Word of God and where the
> Word of God is missing there is no help at all for the soul.[2]

When he was asked how he went about accomplishing the reformation of the church, he said, "I simply taught, preached, wrote
God's Word: otherwise I did nothing. . . . The Word did it all."[3]
There is no alternative resource. There is no experimental diet. The
Word of God feeds the church. Without the Word, the church has
nothing to consume and before long they turn on one another like
the Donner Party.

The Word of God in the church is grounds for happiness; its
absence is a great distress. Maybe we need to be reminded why we
read it together.

The Word Is Elemental

When I was a little boy, I used to like to smash rocks with a hammer.
I think that's the first mode of scientific discovery: smashing. You
don't understand something until you hit it with a hammer. I pum-
meled those stones to powder, wanting to see what was in there.

So I was amazed when I first learned in school that all matter is
made up of the elements on the periodic table, that there are irre-
ducible components of all matter: *elements.*

There are elements in the Christian faith too, and perhaps most
elemental to Christian worship is reading the Word.

The Westminster Confession begins with a proclamation of the
authority and inspiration of Holy Scripture as the Word of God.
In this important document, one that shapes my own tradition and
many others, the Bible is described as "the Word of God written

. . . given by inspiration of God to be the rule of faith and life." The Bible is the collection of Holy Scriptures inspired by God and imbued with "infallible truth and divine authority," as the authors of the Westminster Confession put it so many years ago.[4]

In this book called the Bible, which we can buy and hold in our hands or download to our phones, we don't have a collection of ancient wisdom, a journal of historical events or a collection of poetry—although it contains those things. We have much more than that. We have the very Word of God speaking with divine authority. We can receive it ourselves. Anyone can pick it up and read.

And when we do, with the movement of the Holy Spirit in us, *we hear from God*.

What does the Bible say about itself?

"From childhood," Paul wrote to his protégé Timothy, "you have been acquainted with the sacred writings," the Old Testament, "which are able to make you wise for salvation through faith in Christ Jesus" (2 Timothy 3:15). Paul goes on to say to Timothy— hardly knowing the significance of what he is writing because the Gospels and Paul's own letters would soon fall into this same category—this quintessential claim, "All Scripture is breathed out by God and profitable for teaching, for reproof, for correction, and for training in righteousness" (2 Timothy 3:16).

All Scripture. That must mean every verse and even every word. It isn't only penned by humans but is claimed to be God-breathed— sourced in God himself. Every jot and tittle shares the same authority (Matthew 5:18). From "In the beginning" to "Amen," from Genesis to Revelation, there is not a verse, not a word, that fails to carry the authority of God by his own inspiration in the power of the Holy Spirit.

All Scripture is breathed out by God. God breathed. This is one word in the Greek: *theopneustos*. It means, literally, "blown out," breathed out by God. It's a very intimate word. It reminds us of when Adam was created out of mud and God breathed life into his nostrils. This book isn't distant from God. It is not the sum of our groping attempts to understand the transcendent or to reach toward God from the confines of earth. This book is the expression of God, from God's own core and breath and being, coming from where he is to where we are. That's the Bible.

The Bible is an extraordinary gift of God. To have it is a blessing. To hold and receive the Word of God is itself a source of thanksgiving, awe and joy.

A Gift to Make Us Happy

Each year many churches recognize Pentecost Sunday. We typically think of Pentecost as the birthday of the Christian church because on Pentecost the Holy Spirit blew on the believers and filled the people with power to be the church on God's mission in the world (Acts 2).

But Pentecost was first and is still a Jewish celebration—the celebration of the gift of the five books of the Torah. You might think it's funny to hold a festival to celebrate the books of Genesis through Deuteronomy, but when the God who created the universe hands you the user's manual so that you don't have to stumble around wondering how things work anymore, it is cause for celebration.

And celebrate they did. In fact, it could be a pretty raucous party in first-century Jerusalem. There was wine, dancing and feasting as people came from all nations to celebrate in Jerusalem. That's why Peter explains to the crowd that the followers of Jesus "are not drunk, as you suppose" (Acts 2:15), since it was only nine in the morning. Presumably some others were. Pentecost is the celebration that God gave us the first five books of the Bible as a gift. It's a festival of the Word.

One year I visited with the rabbi of the temple across the street from our church on what happened to be the Jewish Pentecost. He took me into the temple to see a few things. He showed me a Torah scroll recovered from a temple destroyed by the Nazis—a Holocaust scroll they treasured. Then he showed me the collection of Torah scrolls they keep locked in the ark behind the *bimah* of the worship space. They are rolled up on poles and kept in ornate cloth bags. He offered to read a bit for me and took out a scroll. It was made of antelope hide. They don't touch the hide but point at the words and read along holding an ornate silver implement called a *yad*. He read for me, even singing a little bit in Hebrew. Then he rolled up the scroll, bagged it, kissed it and returned it to its place. I felt a little guilty about the Bible I had rolling around the floor in the backseat of my car!

The Word of God is a precious gift.

It is no accident that the Holy Spirit poured over the church on Pentecost. The Spirit and the Word are united. The Holy Spirit accompanies the Word of God. The Word of God is inspired by the Spirit, as 2 Timothy 3:16 reminds us. The breath of God is behind the words of Scripture. But perhaps even more important, the Spirit continuously accompanies the Word of God.

The power of the Holy Spirit descended on the church, granting the apostles the ability to preach, to proclaim the Word of God. The same happens today. The Holy Spirit carries the Word of God along.

It works much in the same way as when we talk to someone. First, we think about what we want to say, then we bring those words into shape by moving our mouth and breathing them out. We have to use breath from our lungs to do this. We draw breath and exhale it to speak, and the breath carries the words through space and time and into our friend's ears so he or she can hear them and get them into his or her own head. So, a word originating in our own mind is transferred, communicated, to another (unless our friend is too busy texting or checking Facebook). That's how it works, in general. The breath accompanies the words.

It is the same with the Word of God. These words, the Bible, are accompanied by the living breath of God, the Spirit. That's how God is able to use these words to speak to us. When we read these words and the Holy Spirit attends them, we begin to hear not some old book from ancient history but God.

The Spirit accompanies and attests to the Word of God given by God as a gift. This gift can be carried by the Spirit into any tongue and language. English is not the home language of the Bible. In Jesus' day there was no English language, nor would there be for hundreds of years! But the Spirit carried the Word into English, and the Spirit carries the Word into Arabic and German and Spanish and Swahili. The Word of God is an unchanging gift to all nations. It is a gift to make us glad.

No Anchor Like the Word

Can't anything simply stay the same? Some years ago I remember taking my wife around my hometown of Colorado Springs to show her my old haunts. The ice-skating rink where my friends and I used to loiter was gone. The favorite pizza place downtown was closed and replaced. Even my high school was unrecognizable, it had been totally renovated.

"I'd love to show you where I grew up, but I can't seem to find it!" I said.

Luckily one little baseball field was still there. It was the sight of my famous game-winning grand slam when I was twelve. My kids groan every time we drive by it.

"Kids! That's where daddy hit the game-winning . . ."

"We know! We know! Quit it, Dad!"

Somehow even that field seems to change. It looks a little smaller every time I drive by. When I hit that home run, it must have traveled a half-mile, but now the outfield is much shorter. I'm not sure how that happened.

Nothing stays the same in this world.

Into this changing, transient world, God reveals his Holy Word, which never changes. Not only does it reveal the heart of God, not only does it show us the intent of our Creator in setting up the universe we dwell in, not only does it convey to us the message of salvation and everlasting life, but it never changes.

This is one more way the Word of God is a gift. It's a rock and an anchor. "The grass withers, the flower fades, but the word of our God will stand forever" (Isaiah 40:8). What anchor is there like the Word? What unshifting foundation can we find greater than the Word of God?

Our faith is not built on shifting sands or perishable things, "not of perishable seed but of imperishable, through the living and abiding word of God" (1 Peter 1:23). When all around us is tumult and change, what greater gift is there than the unchanging Word of God to make us glad?

> **What anchor is there like the Word? What unshifting foundation can we find greater than the Word of God?**

When philosophers and linguists attempt to define *joy*, *gladness* and *happiness*, they return repeatedly to the idea of well-being and security. Joy seems to be connected to a confidence in our own well-being now and security into the future. When everything around us is in constant flux, security is difficult to know. The unchangeableness of the Word of God becomes a dry place to stand in a muddy field, a solid rock in a turbulent river, a harbor from the storm. There is joy and gladness in knowing the solidity of the Word.

The Implanted Word to Save Our Soul

If words are so important, why is an entire language developing to get around using them? Let me run a few by you so you see what I mean: LOL, TTYL, WRYD, BRB, FWIW and ROTFL.[5] I have to look these up because they pop up in my kids' Instagram accounts. I find myself looking at entire paragraphs of information— and I have no idea what it means!

Words do matter, even when they only get one capital letter in a text stream. They are not an inconvenience to work around as quickly as possible. Words are powerful.

You undoubtedly remember some of the words from your childhood. Maybe you overheard some mean girls talking about you or the cool guys dogged you out in the hallway, or maybe a teacher came down too hard on you. The words they used reside in your memory. Words connect us. Soul to soul, mind to mind. There are words that curse, but there are also words that bless. There are even words that save.

> What does it say? "The word is near you, in your mouth and in your heart" (that is, the word of faith that we proclaim); because, if you confess with your mouth that Jesus is Lord and believe in your heart that God raised him from the dead, you will be saved. (Romans 10:8-9)

> How then will they call on him in whom they have not believed? And how are they to believe in him of whom they have never heard? And how are they to hear without someone preaching? . . . So faith comes from hearing, and hearing through the word of Christ. (Romans 10:14, 17)

Words are vital, critical, crucial; words are vehicles of salvation.

God moves in power in the community of faith to reach the fallen, jealous, broken world with the words of life by the power of the Holy Spirit that they too may call on the name of the Lord and be saved. These are the words of life, and they fill the happy church.

Words come to us through the mind. This is an intellectual exercise. But often we get the impression that Christianity is not about the intellect, that Christianity isn't about head knowledge but only heart knowledge. That is, it's not about knowing so much as believing and feeling—we just feel it. This couldn't be further from the truth.

We do not limit Christianity to the realm of feelings. As church scholar Robert Louis Wilken writes, "Christian faith is a matter of the mind as well as the heart and the will, and as thinking persons we must give intellectual expression to our faith."[6]

Christian faith is intellectual as well as emotional. Sometimes we say, "I knew it up here [head], but I needed the Spirit to move it down here [heart]." I understand that. Knowledge of God needs to move from the head to the heart. The truth of God must move us emotionally if it is going to come home in our soul. But it *begins* with the mind. We have to have something in our head to move down to our heart. Something solid. Something true.

Christianity is an intellectual faith. Salvation depends on knowledge of God. Faith is not convincing ourself to believe what we know is not true. Faith is a sure and certain knowledge that what God reveals in Jesus Christ is true. This faith can then seek understanding and follow up the conviction of faith with the surety of knowledge.

In any meaningful and permanent transformation of a person, the mind must be involved. In fact, it must lead the way. What you know determines how you feel. Head rules heart. Knowledge determines feelings and emotions. Volition, the will, derives from knowledge-determined emotions. What we think determines what we want determines what we do, and so follow all the actions that define us as human beings. Or, put another way, what you think determines who you are.

It is a particular gift God have to humans—we are able to think about what we *think* about!

Psychologist Henry Cloud calls this the "executive function" of the human brain. We get to determine where we pay attention:

> Brain researchers say that "attention" is the magic key that unlocks higher-order brain circuitry. When we pay attention to something, repeatedly, the necessary wiring is formed that makes it possible for us to learn new things, take the right actions, and achieve our goals.[7]

A human in perfect balance is ruled by the mind, which runs in the order of knowledge, then feelings and then will. Or, going back the other direction, the things we decide to do are motivated by our feelings, and our feelings are driven by our knowledge (accurate or inaccurate) of the facts. But in our fallen state, this is turned upside down. The body leads the way.

We drive by the Chick-fil-A and see the familiar red sign and our body responds, "Hmm. Tummy want chicken sandwich! Tummy need chocolate shake!" Before you know it, the car has pulled into a drive-through lane.

That's how most of life seems to be lived these days. The body drives the actions, led by desires, and the poor mind is left at the back of the bus trying to make sense of it all after the fact.

"The desires of the flesh are against the Spirit," Paul wrote, "and the desires of the Spirit are against the flesh, for these are opposed to each other, to keep you from doing the things you want to do" (Galatians 5:17). We are dragged around by our bodies' desires. But it doesn't have to be that way.

The Word of God is the tool to turn what is upside down right-side up again. What if the Spirit of God could use the Word of God to infuse our mind with such knowledge of his glory and splendor, such penetrating insight, that suddenly the whole order is flipped upright again, so that now our mind is suddenly confident again to govern our affections?

What if the illuminating power of the Word of God in our mind is enough to give our intellect the confidence to restrain and re-order our desires according to our knowledge of God's own values? What if our mind has the power to control and subdue our body, to alter our habits, change our ingrained activities, to alter our trajectory and propel our whole self, body and soul, in a Christward direction once again? What if that could happen? What if the Spirit-infused human mind could actually take the reins again over the desires and actions of the heart and body? We would be transformed. We would be saved. We might even find peace.

It begins with the mind focused on the Word. Dallas Willard writes in *Renovation of the Heart,*

> As we first turned away from God in our thoughts, so it is in our thoughts that the first movements toward the renovation of the heart occur. Thoughts are the place where we can and must begin to change. There the light of God first begins to move upon us through the word of Christ, and there the divine Spirit begins to direct our will to more and more thoughts that can provide the basis for choosing to realign ourselves with God and his way. The ultimate freedom we have as human beings is the power to select what we will allow or require our minds to dwell upon.[8]

So much of who we are is beyond our control. We can't pick our body. We can't pick our family. We can't choose our own past—even though we did pick much of it for ourselves through our choices, we can't go back and change it.

All of those things make us who we are today, and we can't select any of it freely. But we can decide what we think about. And that is a profound opportunity.

This is surely what James was talking about when he implored us to "receive with meekness the implanted word, which is able to

save your souls" (James 1:21). When we bend our minds toward
Christ by receiving and meditating on his holy Word, we will surely
make progress toward him. That's
the power of the knowledge of
God in you.

> **When we bend our minds
> toward Christ by receiving and
> meditating on his holy Word, we
> will surely make progress
> toward him.**

How to Read Your Bible Together (with Joy)

There is no end of advice on how
to read the Bible. The point of this book is to help the church re-
cover joy. The Word of God is a gift to the people of God, as we
have seen. Its reading and reception should breed gladness, even if
at times it first drives us to despair or challenges us to harrowing
tasks. Even when Scripture challenges us, it is a good gift and
brings great joy. Read it for joy.

Churches tend toward two errors. One is the diminution of the
Word. Its authority is so eroded by qualification after qualification
we are left with the impression that if it could, the church would
walk away from the Scriptures altogether. But the other is the
angry and militaristic relationship with the Word. A church can
fall into a pattern of reading the Bible to find reinforcements for
its defensive positions. Neither of these patterns unleashes the joy
of consuming the Word of God. Let me offer four tips to help us
be joyful readers of Scripture within our communities of faith.

First, when reading the Bible, read it as God's Word and pray
for understanding. The great gift of the Bible is that we can read it!

We can receive it and hear from God. We don't merely read the
Bible to gain ammunition. Sometimes we are so intent on defending our positions that we read only to fill the magazines and
powder kegs so we are ready to fire at the next opponent. On the
other side, we must guard against a hermeneutic of suspicion. It's
easy to get sucked into every controversial claim and erode our

trust in God's Word. Read simply and joyfully, with gratitude that God is speaking to us and with humility so that we might "receive with meekness" (James 1:21) and respond with joy.

We should take the first meaning first, the plain sense, and resist jumping to an interpretation we once heard that explains everything away. Don't assume that what we are reading can't be what it means because it would go counter to the trends of culture, the general morality of the times, or our own predilections and tendencies. Remember it is the Word of God and is meant to confront us, bringing the light of God into our darkened minds, for we are in need of divine instruction. By receiving the Word together we are taught God's own values, not reinforced in our own.

We ought to read the Bible plainly, accepting what it says.

Second, use tools of trusted scholarship to understand the context and original intent of what is read. When was this Scripture written? What was going on in the life of the writer, and what was God doing by inspiring this Word at that particular time? This will help us to not pull a text out of context and misapply it.

John Stott taught the "double authorship of the Bible," meaning he believes it is written by humans *and* by God. Both must be remembered.

> The double authorship of the Bible will affect the way in which we read it. Because it is the word of men, we shall study it like *every* other book, using our minds, investigating its words and syntax, its historical origins and its literary composition. But because it is also the Word of God, we shall study it like *no* other book, on our knees, humbly, crying to God for illumination and for the ministry of the Holy Spirit, without whom we can never understand his Word.[9]

We can read and study these words as they run on the page. But at the same time we must never forget that they are uniquely the inspired Word of God. For this reason we let Scripture interpret Scripture. When stuck on an issue, look within the Bible for the explanation of the Bible. Since it is the inspired Word of God, we must stay within it and under it even as we interpret it, "rightly dividing the word of truth" (2 Timothy 2:15 KJV).

There is no use asking a rabbit how to play Monopoly. We wouldn't ask someone who knows only German to write our English paper. Divine things must be dealt with by divine things. Only in this way can we discern the meaning and "whole counsel of God" on an issue.

Third, when we read, we take Jesus into account. This is understating it a bit. The Bible is the Word written, Jesus is the Word incarnate. So in all we read, we look through the lens of Jesus Christ. Did Jesus sustain or fulfill the teaching in question?

Why don't we eat kosher? Because Jesus said it is not what goes into the body but what comes out that makes us unclean.

Why don't we stone disobedient lawbreakers? Because Jesus took the capital punishment of the law onto himself and took all the wrath of God so that we, disobedient as we are, might experience the love of God.

Why don't we sacrifice animals in the temple? Because Jesus is our high priest who offered once and for all the complete and perfect atoning sacrifice for our sins.

Jesus didn't destroy the Old Testament teachings but fulfilled them, revealing their true meaning and authority. Read the Bible through the lens of Jesus Christ.

Fourth, and most importantly, obey it. Read the Word with the intent to hear and obey. God's injunctions are for his glory and for our well-being.

I once heard pastor Tony Evans put it well. Are you having trouble with the Bible? You say, "Pastor, I don't have confidence in the Bible because I don't understand it all." "Well," he says, "do you understand any verse of it?" "Yeah, I guess." "Then obey that verse, and see where that gets you."

One verse of Scripture obeyed is of greater value in our relationship with God than a thousand verses understood and ignored.

A church pursuing radical joy together will encourage us to try a verse of Scripture on, to obey rather than dismiss the Word of God. The Westminster Catechism sums it up best:

> How is the Word of God to be read? The Holy Scriptures are to be read with an high and reverent esteem of them; with a firm persuasion that they are the very Word of God, and that he only can enable us to understand them; with desire to know, believe, and obey, the will of God revealed in them; with diligence, and attention to the matter and scope of them; with meditation, application, self-denial, and prayer.[10]

We learn to read together with joy in the community of faith. Remember that the gift of teaching, like all spiritual gifts, is bestowed "for the common good" (1 Corinthians 12:7). Our ability to read and understand the Word of God is not simply for our own well-being but "to equip the saints for the work of ministry, for building up of the body of Christ" (Ephesians 4:12).

We used to have a saying among my friends pursuing doctoral degrees in theology: "There's no spiritual gift of sitting around being smart." It's the spiritual gift of *teaching* that edifies the church and adds joy.

Have you've ever met a know-it-all? They can be trying. But a run-of-the-mill know-it-all is nothing compared to a Bible know-it-all. Nothing wrecks a small group or class like the person who has read their Bible as ammo.

At the end of a discussion of one of the most delicate topics Paul takes up with the church at Corinth, he closes with this injunction: "If anyone is inclined to be contentious, we have no such practice,

nor do the churches of God" (1 Corinthians 11:16). We simply don't
sell that here!

On the other hand, there are few joys like the first time someone
finds a Bible verse to help someone else. A woman came up to me
after church a few weeks ago saying, "You told us to memorize a
verse. I did it. You wouldn't believe what happened. That very day
my daughter called in distress, and I quoted the verse I had just
memorized that morning! That was the perfect verse for the
moment. It was just what she needed." It was the first time she had
ever had the Bible verse on hand to give to another as a gift.

What fun it was to see her smile.

Everything We Need

Better to have it and not need it than to need it and not have it.
This is exactly the phrase that fills my shopping cart every time I'm
at the Bass Pro Shops. It feels good to be equipped. Do I need a
collapsible cup with gradated measurements that can double as a
Frisbee? Maybe not right now. But I could need it one day. Better
to have it. It feels good to be equipped.

I remember preparing for our first field exercise in my platoon in
basic training. I had joined the Army Reserve and was being trained
at Fort Jackson, South Carolina, on basic soldier skills. Our drill
sergeants led us through a painfully pedantic process of packing our
rucksacks. Every item was folded exactly the same way and placed
in exactly the same pocket in exactly the same order. It took hours,
and I figured it was little more than one more mind-control ex-
periment. Then the drill sergeant said, "Now, when a soldier gets
hurt, lying in the mud and rain, where is his poncho?" Oh. The back
left cargo pocket. We were ready. We were equipped. Actually, I
have never again felt that feeling of being exactly equipped, of
having exactly what I needed and nothing that I didn't. I suppose
centuries of soldier experience produced a few good ideas.

How much anxiety in your church comes from a general feeling that the church is not equipped? What if you could genuinely say, genuinely believe, "Our church has been given everything it needs to be faithful to Christ today." There is happiness in that. And it is true.

The happiness of the church is often dependent on whether it is being equipped with the Word of God. Sometimes I think it is more dependent on this one question than any other.

How often do you hear a friend explain why she has left her church to seek another, saying, "I just wasn't getting fed there." It's easy to criticize and reply that a mature believer needs to know how to feed on the Word of God herself, and if she is not getting fed at her church, maybe it's time to lead the way in feeding herself and others by taking on some leadership or responsibility. Maybe. But maybe she really wasn't getting fed.

The happiness of the church is often dependent on whether it is being equipped with the Word of God. Sometimes I think it is more dependent on this one question than any other.

Nothing creates anxiety like hunger.

When a church seems unhappy or falls into a crisis, too often the leaders expend all their energy addressing the source of unrest. In the meantime, no one attends to the feeding trough. The sheep get anxious when the hay runs out. Jesus is the good Shepherd. Those in his care do not want for anything because he leads them to good pastures and still waters.

If you are a shepherd of a church, happy or unhappy, do not neglect the feeding trough. Keep leading your people to the Word, where they are fed and equipped. Jesus asked Peter, "Do you love me?" When Peter said yes, Jesus responded, "Feed my sheep" (John 21:17).

The church needs to be equipped. The happy church feels well-equipped and well-fed. All the leaders God sends into the church are bent toward that purpose: "He gave the apostles, the prophets, the evangelists, the shepherds and teachers, to equip the saints for the work of ministry, for building up the body of Christ" (Ephesians 4:11-12).

Get your people fed on the Word of God.

Why do we gather and read the Word of God? Because it is the way God convicts, transforms and equips us to be the church in this world. We consume the Word, and it satisfies us. And this is more than enough to make us glad.

God's Instrument of Praise

What we sing says something significant about
who we are—and whose we are.

JAMES K. A. SMITH

• • •

Every time we sing, three things happen. First, God enjoys the resonance of his own glory in our worship and praise. Second, we feel joy as we fulfill our purpose as God's creatures, which is to reflect his glory in all we do. Third, the lost in the world hear a song they are missing. Like a distant bagpipe in the mountain mist, they hear a tune they thought they knew once—a siren song drawing them toward something they have always longed for. The lost hear the song of home.

Think of your church as an instrument of praise in the hands of God.

The blessings of God feed the roots of happiness for the Christian individually as well as collectively, as the body of Christ. And in its happiness, this body, this happy church redeemed by Christ, has always done one unique thing together: it sings.

The happy church sings.

Some sing like angels while others merely make a joyful noise. Either way, we need to sing.

It has always been the unique character of the Christian church to sing. Where else do you go every week and get asked to break out in song? We don't sing at work, in the mall, at traffic court, in the gym or the supermarket. But at church we sing.

Karl Barth, the Swiss theologian from the twentieth century, wrote about the importance of singing in the church. For him, it was a marker—a sign—of a genuine church. In the days when Nazism infected the church, it was critical to find markers of genuine community. If a gathered community is actually a church, Barth argued, then it expresses itself in praise to God. As he put it, such a community desires to bind itself to God, to commit itself to God, and therefore it strives to express this commitment in the highest and most passionate forms of human communication. In its speech, it doesn't just talk about God; it talks *to* God in deep prayer and *with* God in its preaching. In its singing, it doesn't just sing Christian songs; it worships and praises God with singing in the joy of his presence.

> The Christian community sings. It is not a choral society. Its singing is not a concert. But from inner, material necessity it sings. Singing is the highest form of human expression. It is to such supreme expression that the *vox humana* is devoted in the ministry of the Christian community.[1]

It is part of being a church to sing. It takes great energy, great devotion, and great commitment to sing and to sing well, as anyone devoted to choir or praise bands knows. There is hard work and sacrifice before there is a beautiful song. The true and living church, or as Barth likes to call it, "the community," is the people of God gathered by the Holy Spirit in the joy and confidence of the victories of Jesus Christ. This community will *sing*. It is not a question of choosing whether or not it happens. If the community gathered is in fact the church of Jesus Christ, it will sing.

And it will sing with joy. Barth goes on to say,

The community which does not sing is not the community. And where it cannot sing in living speech, or only archaically in repetition of the modes and texts of the past; where it does not really sing but sighs and mumbles spasmodically, shame-facedly and with an ill grace, it can be at best only a troubled community which is not sure of its expectation.[2]

The Christian church sings. If it can't sing, then something is wrong. If there's no song in its heart, then this community—whatever it is—is not the community gathered and redeemed by Christ. It is not the church. It is something else. If we know Christ, we'll sing.

We won't just mumble old songs either. The church must guard against the tendency to be faithful to the past but empty to the present. Even when we sing the great old hymns, handed down from one generation to the next, we sing them with renewed and fresh joy, always guarding against the temptation to let our songs go dry. The community redeemed by Christ sings from the heart with songs it can sing in its present hour, new songs and old songs, songs that move the body and soul with joy and gladness.

The happy church sings today because it knows its future to-morrow; it knows and expects and is assured that tomorrow is the victory of Christ.

We Are the Strings of God's Instrument

Singing in every worship gathering was a part of the Christian church from the beginning. Jewish worship included some singing, particularly as pilgrims would walk up to Jerusalem for the Day of Atonement. Then, they would sing the Psalms of Ascents (Psalms 120–134). The Levites would also sing as they burned the sacrifice on the altar.[3] There were other cults and societies that sang at this time, but they sang mysterious dirges and mantras. Christians sang every time they gathered, and they sang happy songs. Even as they gathered in the catacombs.

One church father, Athanasius of Alexandria, wrote to a friend around AD 340 that God wants us to sing the psalms and other songs because by this habit "it will be preserved that we love God with our whole strength and power."

Athanasius explained the importance of singing this way: "As in music a [pick] brings out the sound of multiple strings, so the man becoming himself a stringed instrument and devoting himself completely to the Spirit may obey in all his members and emotions, and serve the will of God."[4]

He pictured the church as an instrument in the hands of God. Imagine the church as a stringed instrument, and God is picking it up to play. But for that to happen, each of us must submit ourselves to become the strings. We must allow ourselves to be stretched out in God's hands, drawn across the bridge and fingerboard, and tuned to one another in accordance with the perfect ear of our Master. This singing is a kind of submission before God that brings the soul into harmony. This commitment to worship is an act of selfless abandonment to God, a self-giving. The body, the mind, the soul, all are involved in offering oneself to God in song. We become a stringed instrument, and the Spirit is the pick striking the chord in our very being and drawing the song out of the community of faith.

This, Athanasius says, helps to bring a certain order back into our life and to the church body:

> The praising of God in well-tuned cymbals and harp and ten-stringed instrument was again a figure and sign of the parts of the body coming into natural concord like harp strings,

and of the thoughts of the soul becoming like cymbals, and then all of these being moved and living through the grand sound and through the command of the Spirit so that, as it is written, the man lives in the Spirit and mortifies the deeds of the body [Romans 8:13].[5]

Athanasius drew a picture of the church as an instrument of praise, gladly and harmoniously producing the music of God in the world. That's the ideal.

What happens at your church?

The Divine Bounce of Singing Praise

Music has a tendency to be a source of conflict in a church. Churches have split over the years due to deep fissures developed over music preference. How can we be the happy church when we have different musical tastes and preferences, when we genuinely believe one form of music will elevate the soul or reach the community more effectively than another? Music can exacerbate generational, racial and national differences, and it is *always* emotional.

Worship is our response to God's glory. It is what I sometimes call a divine bounce. God's glory is revealed over us, hits us from above and bounces back up to heaven from our hearts and souls, which splash just a bit toward the sky. God reveals his glory; we return his praise.

The sermon is a form of worship. The Word is revealed and the sermon responds. But where the sermon is written by one individual, our songs are response by committee! The glory of God is revealed in the church, and together a song is composed; collectively a song is chosen; as a community a song is sung, and so this response requires harmony.

Music is much more difficult than preaching. It demands social unity.

The Bible is clear that singing is a requirement for the community of faith. Colossians 3:16 tells us: "Let the word of Christ dwell in you richly, teaching and admonishing one another in all wisdom, singing psalms and hymns and spiritual songs, with thankfulness in your hearts to God." In the same way Ephesians 5:18-20 says,

> Do not get drunk with wine, for that is debauchery, but be filled with the Spirit, addressing one another in psalms and hymns and spiritual songs, singing and making melody to the Lord with your heart, giving thanks always and for everything to God the Father in the name of our Lord Jesus Christ.

When we gather, we are supposed to sing.

These Scriptures have a pattern. There are three similarities we need to pay attention to.

First, isn't it interesting that singing is compared to drunkenness? Peter had a similar problem on Pentecost Sunday in Acts 2. He had to tell the crowd looking in on the Spirit-filled church, "These people are not drunk, as you suppose, since it is only the third hour of the day" (Acts 2:15). The Spirit moved them so much at 9 a.m. that the people around them thought they were drunk. The ancient world commonly associated singing with drunkenness. But for Christians there is no need to drink. We have no need to devolve into debauchery because our happiness in Christ is already a party. So we sing. The Spirit fills the church with such happiness, such deep gladness, that we pursue singing as boldly as drunken sailors!

Is your church singing with that much passion? Are *you*? If not, maybe you need to feel the Spirit a little more than you have been, and let yourself go in communal worship.

Second, these Scriptures connect singing with thanksgiving. When we consider what God has done for us, we overflow with gratitude. John Ortberg writes, "More gratitude will not come from acquiring more things or experiences, but from more of an awareness of God's presence and his goodness."[6] It's tempting to imagine we'll be happier and more thankful when we acquire more stuff. Not so. We become thankful by thinking about God and what he has already done for us.

In *One Thousand Gifts* Ann Voskamp says, "True saints know that the place where all the joy comes from is far deeper than that of feelings; joy comes from the place of the very presence of God."[7] The presence of God produces gratitude; gratitude fills our hearts with joy overflowing in songs of gladness.

Third, these passages repeat the phrase, "psalms and hymns and spiritual songs." I know what a psalm is. There are 150 of them. But what did Paul mean by differentiating "hymns" and "spiritual songs"? I don't know, and we can only guess. But one thing is clear: our singing should have variety. We don't need one type of song. We need many types of songs: psalms, hymns and spiritual songs all alike training our souls to rejoice.

If the divine bounce is a splash of the soul, why shouldn't it be a little messy? Music by nature demands order and discipline, measurement and rehearsal. There is no such thing as a messy song. But the variety of singing in the church is a marker of the divine bounce, splashing in every direction. Naturally, it produces diversity and variety. Why would a Ghanaian sing like a Swede? Why should a ten-year-old sing like a baroque chamber singer if it doesn't resonate in his soul? The splash of worship can go up in an infinite variety of directions.

Much of the conflict over music can be solved by cultivating a generous spirit of joy, wonder and selfless humility in our worship as we grow to be genuinely more concerned for others than for ourselves. Frankly, if we can get this right in our singing and worship, it will bleed into every other aspect of church life.

Worship is the very purpose of the church; get it right and everything else will fall into place. Build it on a foundation of self-
serving preferences and prideful performance, and no part of the
church will find health.

**Worship is the very purpose
of the church; get it right
and everything else will
fall into place.**

Not only should there be a
vivid diversity and variety in the
songs we sing, but the church
should expect its songs to change
over time. This is the way with
music. If it is a genuine expression
of the gathered community of faith today, it will be different from
what it was yesterday, and today's best are tomorrow's memories.

It has always been this way in the church. Professor Hughes
Oliphant Old studied how Reformers like Martin Luther and
John Calvin updated the music for their churches during the Prot-
estant Reformation. They wrote hymns themselves and often used
tunes that emerged from contemporary life—even some drinking
songs. This was all to keep the ministry of praise fresh and alive in
their time, since the older songs had lost their edge. Old writes,

> This often happens to even the best of music; people simply
> get tired of it. Those who sing it get tired of it, and those who
> hear it get tired of it. The music was not bad as much as it was
> stale. The Reformation was amazingly successful in refreshing
> the praises of the Church.[8]

Not all songs go stale. Some are timeless. Many of the best
hymns still sung have risen to popularity over generations or even
centuries. "Phos Hilaron" is thought to be the very first popular
Christian praise song emerging in the first or second century, and
it is still sung. "Amazing Grace" is likely to be sung at funerals
long past my own, and, as one friend remarked, "If I walk in on
Reformation Sunday and the opening hymn is anything other

than 'A Mighty Fortress Is Our God,' I just turn around and walk right back out!"

But treasures like these only wash ashore once in a thousand tides. For the most part music needs constant updating and continuous refreshing—hymns and psalms and spiritual songs in all their variation and vivid creativity. The church should resist the tendency to marry one song or one mode of music for all time. Music is to be sung by the church today, for the church today, and it will not long tolerate singing for yesterday's church.

Let the church sing freely with joy in whatever mode suits, as long as it sings.

Create Something Beautiful

Music in the church is worship by committee. We have to learn how to make something together. Maybe there are gifts in your church, people who have the ability to compose and write music. You don't have to be a composer to make music in church. Often the hard work of creation is simply the sacrifice and commitment of volunteers to produce a beautiful moment in worship to the glory of God, the self-sacrifice among the members of the praise team or choir, giving of their time week by week to be shaped into a harmonious instrument of praise. Music is something beautiful every church makes.

The happy life is not only about knowing God but also being used for his glory. The happy life wants to be used by God to create something beautiful.

There are two types of ambition: to *take* something and to *make* something. God has created us in his image, and we have creative impulses and gifts. We have minds and wisdom to manipulate the world around us and fashion beauty. That's why we make music—God made us capable of it, and we do it for his glory. Singing reminds us we are a creative people, made in the image of God our Creator.

Andy Crouch says we are "culture makers." We Christians are very good at critiquing the world around us, as though we could withdraw from our culture and examine it from afar, rendering our sublime judgments on its virtues and vices. We judge, we critique, we criticize and condemn, but eventually we have to create. Eventually we have to make something. Make something beautiful.

Crouch believes we need to learn much more about how to make something beautiful than how to judge something foul. We must learn to be "gardeners and artists," "cultivators and creators" who are "prepared to both conserve culture at its best and change it for the better by offering the world something new."[9]

I can't think of any area of the church where this is worked out more directly, more regularly and with more ferocity than in the church's music and praise. It's an enormous task, and if we are to be a happy church, our music must be addressed with energy and thoughtfulness.

What God has done makes us sing. God loves to see us use our gifts—the gifts he has given us. And we can feel his enjoyment of our gifts. It's a miraculous loop; a divine bounce. God created the gift. He gave us the capacity to make music. God gave us minds to use mathematics, the curiosity to tap into the harmony of the spheres and the tenacity to train ourselves in the creative act of music. We use the gift God created for his glory when we give ourselves to worship and praise, lifting the highest forms of beauty we can possibly create in music. He is pleased, and we feel his smile, making us want to turn again and use our gifts to please him more. Selflessly we give ourselves to the task again; sacrificially, we pour ourselves into the creative act of music and song, summoning everything in us we attain to the highest form of human expression anew. It's not only a divine bounce, it's a glorious loop of glory and praise, and it goes on forever into eternity.

We sacrifice all we are on the altar of praise. But can it be called a sacrifice when it brings us such pleasure? The selfless giving of ourselves to God becomes a godly cycle of joy—a never-ending fount of happiness.

Join the Song of Heaven

Singing in worship is not just about personal preference or taste. We want our church's music to scratch where we itch, to satisfy our needs and make us comfortable. But what if mature Christian discipleship is more about pouring ourselves out into song for the good of the community and the glory of God than having our own needs met? Lay yourself down and join the song of heaven.

When a worship song touches us in church, when the happy church lifts its voice in sacred song, it is so much more than the movement of a popular piece of music. We are joining the chorus of angels in divine worship.

The age-old refrain goes on,

Praise God, from Whom all blessings flow;
Praise Him, all creatures here below;
Praise Him above, ye heavenly host;
Praise Father, Son, and Holy Ghost.[10]

Our song is part of heaven's song. We worship because heaven worships. We sing because the Holy Spirit sings in us and unites our souls with divine worship in heaven. Our worship is also spiritual formation, training for heaven.

When Jesus was born, the angels filled the sky singing, "Glory to God in the highest, and on earth peace among those with whom he is pleased!" (Luke 2:14). The singing of the angels is revealed at the birth of the Christ-child. Singing fills the heavens in Revelation as the elders and saints all lift up harmonious voice, "Great and amazing are your deeds, O Lord God the Almighty!" (Revelation 15:3). Whatever heaven is, it is full of singing.

It seems like whenever the Holy Spirit shows up, songs erupt. And why not? The Holy Spirit brings the presence of God into our hearts, touches our souls and fills us with gifts. The Spirit comes with song, because "God has sent the Spirit of his Son into our hearts, crying 'Abba! Father!'" (Galatians 4:6). The Spirit is inside us sending praise back to the Father from our own hearts.

So, from the very beginning the happy church has had a song to sing. They were happy to sing the psalms, the hymns, the spiritual songs, because "when they sang the Psalms, the Holy Spirit was praising the Father within their hearts."[11]

Singing, worship, it's that important. It is a transforming moment, reshaping us from the inside out. That's why it's so important to get back to church every week and be led in singing praise. It's like a compass whose needle gets stuck—we need the songs of praise to shake the needle of our heart so it points to Jesus again. We let God hold all the strings of our life and strike the chord with his pick. And our lives become a love song.

In Mark's Gospel, after the Last Supper, after the betrayal of Judas, Jesus taught the apostles the most important way they would come together in worship.

> As they were eating, he took bread, and after blessing it broke it and gave it to them, and said, "Take; this is my body." And he took a cup, and when he had given thanks he gave it to them, and they all drank of it. And he said to them, "This is my blood of the covenant, which is poured out for many. Truly, I say to you, I will not drink again of the fruit of the vine until that day when I drink it new in the kingdom of God." (Mark 14:22-25)

And how did they close this holy meal? "And when they had sung a hymn, they went out to the Mount of Olives" (v. 26).

They *sang*!

There are moments together in the life of faith that need a song. Singing together unites us, comforts us, cheers us and supports us through great trials. Singing is not only a gift for us individually, it is a charism for the church—a holy gift meant to be shared.

When we use our gifts in the right way, we feel good, and the people around us feel served and encouraged. We submit to one another as we submit our gifts to God. The song is no different. It is made and offered in thanksgiving, humbly, in submission and service. We sing together.

> **Singing together unites us, comforts us, cheers us and supports us through great trials. Singing is not only a gift for us individually, it is a charism for the church—a holy gift meant to be shared.**

The Song of Happiness

Boethius, a Christian philosopher, studied the human thirst for happiness. He felt the reason we aren't happy, even though we want to be, is that we settle. We don't strive for true happiness hard enough. We expect happiness from particular pursuits, particular conquests we think will make us happy—success at work, accumulation of wealth, satisfying marriage and the like. But happiness eludes us unless all these areas are equally and simultaneously successful. He wrote, "So there is no way in which happiness is to be found in those pursuits which were believed individually to bestow desirable things."[12]

We know we're onto something when the same idea that was true in AD 500 is still true today. We can't find the happiness we want by seeking it in one or two pursuits. We try to make work happen, and family suffers. We try to make family happen, and our hobbies and personal development suffer. When we pursue any one piece of the puzzle with enough passion and commitment to attain happiness in it, and all the other pieces start to fall off the table onto the floor. But the real problem is giving up. The real problem is that we settle for less.

Boethius wrote a poem, and part of it is about a bird in a cage. It was written in Latin, so this is a rough translation:

And the woodland songster, pent
In forlorn imprisonment,
Though a mistress' lavish care
Store of honeyed sweets prepare;
Yet, if in his narrow cage,
As he hops from bar to bar,
He should spy the woods afar,
Cool with sheltering foliage,
All these dainties he will spurn,
To the woods his heart will turn;
Only for the woods he longs,
Pipes the woods in all his songs.[13]

In all his songs there is a melody, a somber tune calling out for the woods where he belongs. The bird's song reminds it that it is not yet home, that it belongs in another land of freedom and satisfied joy. But he gets a lot of sweets in that cage. Probably if the owner left the door open, he wouldn't even dare to venture out.

Maybe we are too easily satisfied with the honeyed sweets of our gilded cage. Maybe we're accepting the lavish care of our mistress, who is actually our keeper. Maybe we're caged and there's plenty around us to keep us comfortable, plenty to keep us occupied. There's always a TV or screen glowing in our eyes. There's plenty of beer in the fridge to keep us sedated. There's plenty of comfort and plush toys and devices and bells—but in our hearts we long to sing a true song.

Every now and then we glimpse the woods. "Only for the woods he longs; / Pipes the woods in all his songs." Our true longing emerges, and we know: we know we will never be happy until we are free again.

God has made his church an instrument of praise. When the song plays, he is glorified and we are gladdened, but one more thing happens. The song of the church is heard by the world, the world that is darkened. The world that is lost in the menagerie of gilded sweets, the distractions of the age. There is something in every human soul that longs to sing the glory of God.

If we, the people of God, resolve to pursue the joy of the Lord in radical and countercultural ways, then we will root our songs in the one true source of beauty. We will root all our songs in the glory of God and cultivate and create and elevate harmonies of praise, not for ourselves but to the resonating worship of God. We won't have time for petty and selfish bickering when the beauty of God is so manifest and weighty before us. And the world will hear our songs of joy.

> **We will root all our songs in the glory of God and cultivate and create and elevate harmonies of praise, not for ourselves but to the resonating worship of God.**

Augustine tells the story of his conversion in *Confessions*. He wrote the book as though speaking to God and said,

> The tears flowed from me when I heard your hymns and canticles, for the sweet singing of your Church moved me deeply. The music surged in my ears, truth seeped into my heart, and my feelings of devotion overflowed, so that the tears streamed down. But they were tears of gladness.[14]

The music of the church in Milan was part of his conversion to Christ. When the church sings its songs faithfully and with joy, the world hears with longing.

I've sung songs with the Christ Church Cathedral Choir in Oxford as I sat in the congregation. I sang along with the "Hallelujah Chorus" at the end of a performance of Handel's *Messiah* in the Sheldonian Theater. I've sung songs with Matt Redman and

Chris Tomlin in the throngs of tens of thousands. But I believe the happiest song I ever sang was in a dirt-floor home in Kikuyu, Kenya. After being hosted for dinner, Abigail and I were seated on the couch and told that the young lady in the house—a shy, sweet girl who was kept in the house by mercy because her own parents could not afford her care—wanted to sing a song for us. She came out, stood before us trembling and began to sing:

God is so good;
God is so good;
God is so good;
He's so good to me.

Five of us there, in a two-room house of left-behind wood and corrugated tin, joined to sing together. I believe it was the most beautiful song I've ever heard, and I can still hear it today. A happy song. A marker of the true church and a banner in the colors of heaven. She gave us a taste of our eternal home, and my heart burned to see the kingdom come.

There is such a song in your church.

We will never be fully satisfied until the song we sing is sung in total devotion, total freedom from the distractions of our gilded cage full of worldly devices. Our hearts long to sing the free song of heaven in the presence of the Lord, the unencumbered chorus of the saints in light, the songs of heaven with a thousand golden-throated angels. That's the song we long to sing. That's the chorus we must join to be free.

5

Prayers of the People

*Prayer is a little like that. With simplicity of heart
we allow ourselves to be gathered up into the arms of the
Father and let him sing his love song over us.*

RICHARD FOSTER

• • •

As soon as she hit send on the text she knew she had made
a mistake. Immediately she called her sister back.

"I'm so, so sorry. I should have asked."

Beth and her sister had just spent an hour on the phone together
crying. Her sister was in crisis mode dealing with a piece of devastating and very private news. But when they hung up, Beth's first
thought was to contact her friends. She texted a group prayer re-
quest without thinking.

"It's my prayer group. I just didn't know what to do other than
ask them to pray. They will keep it private; we keep secrets well for
each other. But, I'm sorry. I really should have asked before I shared
anything at all."

"No, that's okay, I guess," her sister said.

"Are you sure? You sound hesitant."

"Really. I'm sure it's fine."

There was a silent pause. Beth was worried. She didn't mean to break trust with her sister, only to reach out for help in an impossible situation.

But that was not what her sister was thinking about in the pregnant silence.

The silence broke. "You mean you have friends that pray for you?"

We take prayer for granted. If you are a mature Christian, prayer might feel like breathing. But it is a gift.

The practice of prayer increases the happiness of the church. It solves our loneliness, binding us together in community. It connects us to God and the eternal life found in him through Christ. It gives us a sense of purpose and fulfillment when we pray for God's work to be done through us, and we see the results of answered prayer. It is the lifeblood of the church, the soul of the community of faith.

We Are Not Alone

People love their privacy, but they hate their loneliness. For all our social media connections and constant plugging in, people seem to feel more lonely and isolated than in previous generations. Meaningful friendships are on the decline.

Where can you go to build relationships that matter? Who can you trust with your secret pain?

You mean you have friends that pray for you?

Prayer breaks through the isolation. We are not alone when we intimately connect with one another and with God. Prayer is a great gift given to every church and every Christian. In a life marked by love for God and love for neighbor, there is nothing to connect us to God and to one another quite so powerfully as prayer.

> **Prayer breaks through the isolation. We are not alone when we intimately connect with one another and with God.**

The church prays together. For many churches (particularly larger churches) sharing prayer concerns and praying for one another is left to small groups, and little time is given to public prayer during worship. But maybe your church takes time to pray during worship, the prayers of the people. The pain of the community, the pain of the world—it's too much to bear alone, so as the people of God we carry those burdens to church and lay them at the foot of the cross. This time of prayer often ends with the Lord's Prayer, encapsulating all we need to say before the Lord—and we say it "with one voice."

But prayer doesn't only happen in the worship service. Some of the most powerful moments of prayer happen far from the sanctuary or worship space. People stop and pray for one another in the halls and the parking lot. Small groups meet together in homes and share their burdens in confidence. Friendships develop with enough trust to share the actual pain, the actual brokenness in their lives, and so actual prayers can be said.

Prayer pervades the church. The happy church is a church at prayer. Jesus said, "My house shall be called a house of prayer" (Mark 11:17).

In *Life Together*, Dietrich Bonhoeffer wrote that it's important to put away our misgivings and learn to pray together:

> No matter what objections there may be to prayer together, it simply could not be any other way. Christians may and should pray together to God in their own words when they desire to live together under the Word of God. They have requests, gratitude, and intercessions to bring in common to God, and they should do so joyfully and confidently.... It is in fact the most normal thing in our common Christian life to pray together.[1]

It is the most normal thing—normal for us but not normal for the world. Outside of the church, people get by without prayer.

There is tremendous joy in knowing we are not alone, that together we pray and our prayers are heard by God.

Maybe we neglect to enjoy it.

Prayers Connect Us to God

What do outsiders think of the church at prayer? "What are those Christians doing in there?" They must think we do what we do in an effort to please God, trying to get our God to give us what we want. Just like every totemistic religion ever contrived, we pray to please our God in hopes of benefits returned for sacrificial religious behavior.

I hope not. But I fear it is often true

In any given church service, I wonder how many are "trying the God thing" again. Thinking, *Maybe God will notice if I go to church and pray this week, and my stock portfolio will even out* (or *my promotion will come through*, or *my kid will make that team*). But it doesn't work. Prayer is not a method to push God into a corner and force him to bend to our will.

Professor Bing Hunter calls it the "divine vending machine."[2] We are certain that if we could find the right currency we could make it work. Gather up the right mix of good deeds and obedience, insert the credits into the slot, and make your selection. Then, boom! Out pops exactly what you want. We are not trying to conquer God, just get him to return what we think we deserve.

Prayer is not a trip to the divine vending machine. This is not what Jesus meant by "a house of prayer."

Clement of Alexandria put it simply in the early church: "Prayer is conversation with God."[3] What is prayer? It's dialogue with God. It's talking with him. Prayer is intimate conversation between creature and Creator, between a soul and the God who sustains it. In formal terms we recognize prayer as our ability to converse with God on the basis of the communion with God won for us in Jesus Christ. This is an extraordinary gift. God is pleased to talk with us.

Like all conversation, this conversation connects and unites. By prayer, the people of God are united to God in mind, heart and will.

The mind is united to God by Scripture and prayer. God's part of the dialogue is his holy Word, and our part is our rejoinder in prayer. We can't pray effectively to God if we aren't reading his Word. This correspondence shapes our minds after God's mind like nothing else.

The will is also united to God. **We can't pray effectively to God if we aren't reading his Word.** This occurs when we pray with open hearts, revealing our desires. Richard Foster encourages us to pray openly and honestly, not filtering our prayers for appropriate versus inappropriate requests but engaging in "an ongoing conversation with God."[4] "For now, do not worry about 'proper' praying, just talk to God. Share your hurts, share your joys—freely and openly. God listens in compassion and love, just like we do when our children come to us. He delights in our presence."[5]

Our prayers should lay bare the desires of our hearts. That's intimacy. We can speak freely and openly in prayer, showing the Lord what we want, right or wrong. Let your intimate conversation with God be simple, pure and unashamed, and don't worry if you think your desires might be wrong. If you pray openly from the heart, God will reveal your useless desires and change what longings remain to match his perfect goodness.

Prayer also knits our will with God's will. As John Stott taught, "The purpose of prayer is emphatically not to bend God's will to ours, but rather to align our will to his."[6] What we experience as powerful prayer is actually an alignment with the will of God, when we delight in God's will in every area of life. When our will is knit to God's will, we find ourself unleashing the power of God through prayer as our own desires, convictions and passions are united with the movement of the Spirit of God to save, heal and redeem this broken world.

The more we pray, the more our mind is knit to God's mind, our heart is knit to God's heart, our will is knit to God's will, and we find we want to *do* differently. The will of God subsumes our own will; our own will becomes aligned to the will of God. "Thy kingdom come; Thy will be done." Our soul begins to pray, *Let your kingdom come in me, as it comes into the world. Let your kingdom, O Lord, reign in my heart.*

Richard Foster writes, "In prayer, real prayer, we begin to think God's thoughts after him: to desire the things he desires, to love the things he loves, to will the things he wills."[7]

We are not pulling God into our world by prayer; he is pulling us into his.

> **We are not pulling God into our world by prayer; he is pulling us into his.**

Prayer is not a means to an end; it is an end in itself—connecting with God.

The happy church engages in prayer, and by this active conversation with God—not entirely unlike human conversation—our minds are knit to God's mind, our hearts are knit to God's heart, our wills are knit to God's will, and the church is connected to God.

Pray and Watch God Work

Can a church have a mind, heart and will united to God through prayer? Absolutely. I would frame the question in reverse. Can an individual possibly have mind, heart and will united to God in prayer without a church to teach the person how?

When the disciples asked Jesus to teach them how to pray, he taught them a prayer to be said in groups: "*Our* Father, who is in heaven . . ." The primary patterns of prayer Christ teaches are for the people of God to practice together.

God builds his kingdom through his people, using the people of God at prayer to lavish blessings on the world. Time and again Scripture promises that God will move when the people of God pray together. Prayer is the fuel that drives the church. Without prayer there is no propulsion. God moves the church forward by prayer.

John Calvin said God has a storehouse of blessings he will not release until we pray for them. Why? Because if we received these benefits without seeking them fervently from the Lord in prayer, we might get the idea that we had attained them for ourselves by our own effort or fallen on them by blind luck. And the whole purpose of the blessing from God is that it draws us closer to him, the one who blesses. Prayer unleashes God's blessings.

Not to seek the Lord in prayer, said Calvin, is as foolish as leaving treasure buried in a field after someone has pointed out to us exactly where it lies. Even though God often helps us unasked, we are fools to know that whatever we need and whatever we lack is in God but not seek him in prayer.[8]

The people of God in pursuit of radical joy pray together and together celebrate when God moves. It is so much more powerful than praying alone. Alone we can forget that we asked God to move. Alone we are tempted to explain the coincidence away. Alone we succumb to egotism; when someone congratulates us on a great accomplishment we prayed for alone, we might warmly receive the credit, feeding our pride instead of God's praise. But if we have sought God in prayer with others, celebrating God's answers to prayer will be the most natural thing to do.

Prayer always makes a difference; it unleashes blessings because it always brings us closer to God.

Researcher and CEO of LifeWay Christian Resources Thom Rainer touched off a small firestorm last year when he published his book *Autopsy of a*

> **Prayer always makes a difference; it unleashes blessings because it always brings us closer to God.**

Deceased Church, suggesting that a lack of prayer was one of the key indicators of a terminal church.[9] People coming out of the emotional experience of closing their churches responded with anger at the suggestion they had not prayed hard enough. It wasn't that they hadn't prayed. They had. But it seems that the dying churches did not know *how* to pray for the mission of God.

What are you praying for at church? We pray the budget comes in okay. We pray the pipes don't burst. We pray people will stop leaving. We pray our friends' medical procedures will go well. Legitimate concerns, sure. But what about praying for the mission and vision of the church? What about praying down the kingdom?

Jesus told Peter and the disciples that he would build his church and "the gates of hell shall not prevail against it" (Matthew 16:18). As pastor Mark Batterson points out in his book *All In*, gates are defensive battlements. That means the church is on offense, and the powers of hell are trying to defend their positions. Why are we trying to play defense when the Lord sent us out to play offense? No wonder we're having such a hard time![10]

The church is not supposed to be on the defensive. Every piece of the "armor of God" listed for the church in Ephesians 6 is worn on the front of the body, not the back. We are on offense for Christ against the powers of darkness. Let our prayers reflect it. Are we praying on offense or defense?

When the church elevates its mission and pursues Christ with fervor in prayer, hearts, minds and wills start to unite in new ways.

Thom Rainer points to the Acts 2 church: "They devoted themselves to the apostles' teaching and the fellowship, to the breaking of bread and the prayers" (Acts 2:42). They were "devoted" to prayer. That's not a passing interest. In the Old Testament *devoted* is the word used to describe an ox being slaughtered in sacrifice and laid on the altar to be burned! That's devoted! All in. Nothing remains. No holding back.

Is your church *devoted* to prayer?

Jesus explained the mission of the church very clearly. He modeled it himself throughout his ministry and up to his passion and crucifixion. He came "not to be served but to serve, and to give his life as a ransom for many" (Mark 10:45). "For the Son of Man came to seek and to save the lost" (Luke 19:10). He then sent the disciples on the same mission, but told them to wait until power had come on them.

The disciples should know better than to try to carry on without the power of Christ. When they tried to heal a boy (Mark 9), they couldn't do it without the power that comes by prayer. When Peter tried to walk on water, he began to sink without the power that comes from calling out to Christ. The people of God would not move out into the world to be witnesses until the power of the Holy Spirit came over them (Acts 1:8). The power that comes by prayer is what propels the people of God.

The church must learn to pray the mission of God beyond its own concerns for survival. Instead of insular prayers, how about missional prayers? How about praying to sponsor a dozen students to the Passion Conference or Urbana Student Missions Conference or some such gathering? How about praying that God would use your church to rescue a dozen children from forced labor around the world this year by partnering with International Justice Mission? How about praying that God would reach the lost in your neighborhood through your church? Go on offense with your prayers.

The scariest question to ask a church member is, what is your church praying for right now? Not because I fear that they are praying for something terrible, but I fear they don't know what they are praying for at all.

Let's take Thom Rainer's worst case. Let's say your church is in its last year. How do you want to spend it?

I would say burn out in a blaze of glory! Devote it to Christ fully on the altar! Why not? I would rather see every remaining resource spent on the mission to seek and to save the lost than on one more year of institutional survival. Build the kingdom of God with whatever you have left! One soul saved is of infinitely greater value than the building in which it occurs. Go for it!

Hopefully your church is not at such a point of desperation. But what will it take to tip the agenda of your prayers to the mission of God in Christ to seek and save the lost?

Can your church pray bold prayers? Pray offense, and let evil fear losing ground for a change.

One Prayer, Three Miracles

"Before we head home tonight, let's take some time to pray for more students to come." One of our elders was closing a meeting of the Christian education team. They had spent an hour getting updated on the preschool, which had only twelve students after a year of effort. Not much.

The elder recalled that we had talked together in our elder board about how important the preschool was to our mission to reach our community for Christ. Our church is situated in the middle-class North Atlanta suburbs. Everything here centers on kids. We needed a strong outreach for Christ through a strong preschool, but ours was struggling. Losing money fast.

"Lord, we pray that you would use our preschool to help us on this mission you've put us on. Please use us to reach our community for Christ. Please build our preschool," she prayed, "and use it for your glory."

The next morning I met a friend from out of town for breakfast. He wanted to see the church. We drove up to find circles of moms, many with babies on their hips, sobbing in our parking lot. The preschool their children were enrolled in had suddenly and dramatically collapsed. Could they possibly join ours?

Over the weekend, our preschool went from twelve students and three teachers to seventy-five students and twelve teachers.

That was miracle number one.

Then the problems came. Some changes to the facility were necessary, at expense. In particular, a room outfitted by the private donations of a small group who met in it regularly would need to be retrofitted to become a preschool classroom. I was not looking forward to the phone call.

"This is Pastor Tim. I suppose you've heard about the great miracle! We have a full preschool now! Well, there is something I need to ask you. You know how your small group has invested to make room 7 so nice? Thank you for that, by the way, it really is so nice . . ." I was using my most diplomatic voice. "We may need to use that room for preschool students."

I glanced down at my notepad where I had scribbled a few ideas about how to answer possible objections. I braced in the silence and waited for the worst.

"Really?" the small group leader said. "That's exactly what we've been praying for, isn't it? Praise God! Of course we'll move."

Miracle number two.

But neither of those is the real miracle. No, the real miracle was number three. You see, the prayer wasn't, "Can we have a preschool please?" It was, "Would you please use our preschool to reach our community for Christ?" The real miracle came the following year when nearly two dozen of those families came into our church, some of them committing to Christ for the first time. One Sunday, a mother and a child were baptized together.

When the church prays together, it unites with Christ's work in the world to seek and to save the lost, to build the kingdom, to bring good news to the poor, release to captives, sight to blind and liberty to the oppressed (Luke 4:18). When the church prays together it is united in mind, heart and will with the purposes of God. When a church prays together it begins to see what God has in store, why God placed a particular group of believers in a particular place.

It's a small thing, this story of ours. One more church preschool in one more American suburb. This is not a revival story for the history books. But this story can be your story; it can be any church's story that will offer itself, devoted, to the Lord for his purposes in prayer. Who knows what the Lord intends to do with your church when it is all together, devoted to prayer? I can tell you this, you will be happy to see the harvest.

Just as Jesus Prayed

The purpose of prayer is to increase our intimacy in our relationship with God. We ask. He answers. And we grow closer and closer, for "the Lord is near to all who call on him" (Psalm 145:18).

Joy is unleashed in our churches when our communal prayers are understood to connect us intimately to God and what he is doing in the world for his own glory. It's easier to be the happy community of faith with exuberance when we look up from our collective prayers and know that we have all drawn near to the Father in heaven, opening our hearts with genuineness and selfless abandon. We are pulled out of our loneliness into active community, we are connected to God and feel his presence, and our prayers are fulfilled when we see the activity of God connected to our prayer life.

This is exactly what Jesus intended for us; it is exactly what Jesus prayed for us. In John 17 we see Jesus crying out to heaven on behalf of his disciples and followers, the church, to know that they are connected eternally. "Father, the hour has come," he says, just before his arrest and sacrificial death in Jerusalem. "Glorify your Son that the Son may glorify you, since you have given him authority over all flesh, to give eternal life to all whom you have given him" (John 17:1-2).

In his final hours, his most needful and trying moments, Jesus prayed that *we* might receive eternal life. "And *this* is eternal life, *that they know you* the only true God, and Jesus Christ whom you have sent" (John 17:3, emphasis added). No more fake life. No more disappointing life. No more half-full life. Eternal life, overflowing life, fullness of life for now and for eternity is found in knowing God.

At the very pinnacle of his ministry on earth, Jesus prayed for *our* intimacy with God. Jesus prayed for our prayers! Notice something, now. Jesus spoke his prayers for "them," not for him or for her, not for he, she or it, but for "them." Third person plural. The high-priestly prayer of Jesus is for his church, all together. Jesus prayed for the prayers of the church, for the unity of the church, for the eternal life to flow in the church, and for the church to know joy.

Jesus prays, "Now I am coming to you, and these things I speak in the world, that they may have my joy fulfilled in themselves" (John 17:13). Here is the object, the goal of Jesus' prayer—that our joy may be complete. That fullness of joy might abide in his church. That the people of God may be united to Jesus with as much unity as Jesus experiences with the Father, and that this union with Christ might manifest itself in fulfilling, overflowing, completing, exceeding *joy.*

By such a union, and by such joy, there is one more thing to expect: "so that the world may believe. . . . So that the world may know that you sent me and loved them even as you loved me" (John 17:21, 23).

Linked up with one another and united to God, the people of God at prayer begin to see a difference being made. God is making a dent in the darkness by their prayers, shedding light in dark places, reflecting his holy light off the community joined to him in prayer—and the world sees it. Such a union, producing such joy, becomes a witness to the world. That's the prayer of Jesus. That's why we pray. That's how the happy church in prayer becomes a witness to Christ in the world.

Pray and Be Happy

The habitual presence of God produces ecstasy. We learn this joy in community.

Happy is the church that prays to be with Jesus. Happy is the church that learns to pray simply that they might dwell in the ecstasy of the habitual presence of God in Jesus Christ. "Would you be happy?" asked Charles Haddon Spurgeon. "Be much in prayer."[11] Prayer draws us into intimacy with God, and the presence of God is our joy.

I need constant lessons in prayer. Once I was temporarily the pastor of a beautiful little church at the foot of the Blue Ridge Mountains in Crozet, Virginia. There was a woman on the church rolls who could not make it to worship. The elders told me I needed to visit her.

Her name was Mrs. Geneva McDaniel—and that's how everyone referred to her, "Mrs. Geneva McDaniel." Not Geneva. Not Mrs. McDaniel. Mrs. Geneva McDaniel.

I was nervous to visit her. I knew she was stuck in her small apartment, and I knew she was elderly and respected (and maybe a little feared). Her friends in church visited her, but I had put off Mrs. Geneva McDaniel as long as I could, dodging the frightful task until the last week of my interim. What a mistake that was.

The minute I arrived I knew that I was there to receive much more than I would give.

"So you're the young pastor I've been waiting to see. Come in. Sit down."

It was a little dark, but not unfriendly.

"Have a seat. You think I'm alone here, but I'm not."

With those words, Mrs. Geneva McDaniel began to share her faith with me. In the morning, she said, she wakes up and says hello to Jesus. She prays and writes in her journal. Then she opens her Bible to read and pray. She feels the presence of Jesus with her all day long. At the end of the day, when she prepares for sleep, she prays and journals again. She smiled as she told me of the gifts of Jesus she receives daily alone in her chamber with him. She smiled with the ecstasy of the habitual presence of God.

She was such an encouragement to me, and feeling that I was in the presence of wisdom I began opening up and sharing all sorts of doubts and fears with her.

Can you imagine? I went to visit *her*. In comes this young pastor charged with the responsibility of true religion—to visit widows and orphans in their need—and in a few minutes he's tearfully unloading his own burdens!

My life at the time was not as smooth as I had planned it to be. My career plans, my PhD program and my tender life with my young family were all being put on hold because I was preparing to deploy as a chaplain in the Army Reserve. In the openness of that quiet room, I unloaded my burdens to her. What I never said out loud to anyone, I awkwardly spilled on this dear saint: I was scared that I might die.

I started to cry, and I shared with Geneva—excuse me, Mrs. Geneva McDaniel—that when I was young I could give my life to Christ easily. I would just sign it over: "Here you go, Jesus. It's yours."

"But now it's more difficult," I said. "It's not just my life handed over to Christ but my family, my wife, my kids, their lives, and all our common dreams, and all the ways those dreams depend on me as the father and husband."

It was no longer so easy to say I would give my life for Christ's service. It was becoming harder to pray.

Mrs. Geneva McDaniel stopped me.

She smiled and said, "I believe God always has a purpose for us, and he always puts us where he wants us. I believe you were here at our church for a purpose, even though it was a short time, and I believe that God has purposes for you over there if you must go, and he will watch over your family."

Faith. Trust. Born of the constant ecstasy of the habitual presence of God met in prayer day by day, hour by hour. I needed that lesson in prayer again.

You may think that's a story of an individual, but it's not. Nobody prays alone. The joy of communion with God is learned in a church; it is experienced in community first. The fruit of this practice is a woman who knows the joy of the community united to God in prayer even when she is alone.

Like most things we take for granted, we only see the value of prayer in community when it is taken from us.

Dietrich Bonhoeffer taught that Christians ought to pray the psalms in their gatherings. He claimed that in practicing communal prayer and using Psalms as a prayerbook, "I learn to join the body of Christ in its prayer. . . . Is that not meant to be an indication that the one who prays never prays alone?"[12]

When he was locked in a cell toward the end of his life, awaiting his execution, he felt the presence of the community of faith surrounding him supernaturally. He wrote to his fiancée:

> I have had the experience over and over again that the quieter it is around me, the clearer do I feel the connection to you. It is as though in solitude the soul develops senses which we hardly know in everyday life. Therefore I have not felt lonely or abandoned for one moment. You, the parents, all of you, the friends and students of mine at the front, all are constantly present to me.[13]

That was the final letter she received from him.

We are not alone. We pray together even when we are isolated. No cell can contain us. By prayer we scale the walls to connect with our brothers and sisters, to connect with our God, who joins us in our prayers by his Holy Spirit. We never pray alone.

Why do we pray? For us? For our benefit? Sure. But foremost we pray for the presence of God in Jesus Christ to manifest himself in the community of faith. To know the one true God and experience the joy of his salvation together and to see his kingdom burst forth in us. Let's pay a little more attention to our prayer life. Not just alone but as a church. It is a root of happiness in the Lord.

"Would you be happy?" asked Spurgeon. Pray. Seriously, could it possibly be that simple?

There is a people of regular and patterned prayer. They are in pursuit of radical joy in the Lord. The Lord, in fact, has prayed already for them—for the wellsprings of eternal life to overflow in them as they lift the prayers of the people all together. They are gathered up in the joyful lap of the Father, and his love song over them is happiness.

6

Laughing Matters

Really, for a man who had been out of practice for so many
years, it was a splendid laugh, a most illustrious laugh.
The father of a long, long line of brilliant laughs!

CHARLES DICKENS

● ● ●

It's not easy to fight for joy. It's not always easy to laugh. It often seems the case that when we resolve to pursue happiness, to renew our joy in the Lord, great trials come. Great waves come and buffet the side of the ship. Trials and burdens press down like weights. Charles Spurgeon once preached,

> If trials be weights I will tell you of a happy secret. There is such a thing as making a weight lift you. If I have a weight chained to me, it keeps me down; but give me pulleys and certain appliances, and I can make it lift me up. Yes, there is such a thing as making troubles raise me towards heaven.[1]

It's a happy secret. It's a paradox. When our life is attached to Christ on the cross, even things that are supposed to weigh us down become weights on the pulley lifting us toward our heavenly King. It is a beautiful reversal.

Ignatius of Antioch compared the cross to a crane, saying, "You are being carried up to the heights by the crane of Jesus Christ, which is the cross, using as a cable the Holy Spirit; and your faith is your hoist, and love is the path that carries you up to God."[2] This is the secret paradox of the Christian. We can't be pushed down. If we are attached to the cross of Christ by faith, the events and people in life that should push us down serve to drive us closer to Jesus and deepen our joy.

We find deep foundations for happiness in Jesus Christ. The greatest Christian thinkers of all times, stretching from the early church to the present day, agree that true happiness comes from knowing God and being used for his purposes. When we submit ourselves to God in reverent devotion, God crafts us into an instrument of his purposes. God takes over, and we feel his elevation grabbing hold of our lives, making our moments more significant and meaningful. Suddenly, every hardship is filled with meaning. Suddenly, we have a greater appreciation of all things. Our own pattern of life takes the shape of "organizing ourselves around life in God that we may enjoy ourselves as we are buoyed by the love, beauty, goodness and wisdom of God, which hoist us aloft."[3]

> The greatest Christian thinkers of all times, stretching from the early church to the present day, agree that true happiness comes from knowing God and being used for his purposes.

There is a power to hoist us aloft. A power that lifts our spirits in the rising wafts of smoke, the rising waves of the breath of God, lifting our souls in waves of love, beauty, goodness and wisdom. An updraft of the Holy Spirit comes just when it is most needed.

That's when we laugh.

The paradox makes us laugh. The surprising turn, the plot twist. The victory that surprises us when we expected defeat.

Jesus always, always wins! His victories are beautiful and surprising and belong to him alone—and they make us laugh. They make us laugh heartily and fully. Not in a silly way, but rich and deep. The reversal, the turn, the secret joy—we can't help it. It erupts into laughter, and as we are taken into the joy of it we laugh with the one who said, and meant, "Happy are those who mourn" (Matthew 5:4 GNT). Even in the sadness there is happiness.

We are part of the happy church of God, the people who know there is validity to joy, power in happiness, strength to overcome, laughter in the lions' den, and that these things are from God. We are in pursuit of a foundation, bedrock, solid reason to be happy. The happiness we find when we are rooted in Christ—when our deepest roots under the surface reach to Christ as our source—doesn't make sense to the world and can't be overtaken by the hardships of life or by dark powers in this world. The happiness we find rooted in Jesus Christ laughs in the face of death.

There is tremendous spiritual significance to laughter among the people of God. Some take it as a particular gift of the Spirit, a charism known as the enthusiasm of holy laughter for a few. I take it as a gift for us all. Cultivating laughter is vital to the radical pursuit of joy.

What's the Deal with Laughter?

When I was a child, I told my parents I wanted to be a stand-up comedian. The second thing I told them I wanted to be was a boxer, and the third was an astronaut. So I became a pastor! It seems to fit them all.

The serious business of humor is hard work. I'm glad I am not a comedian.

I went to college with Seth Meyers, who was *Saturday Night Live*'s head writer for many years before taking over for Jimmy Fallon in the *Late Night* slot. Sometimes I'm jealous of him. But then I think about actually doing his job—sitting down every morning to an empty sheet of paper and thinking of something funny to say in front of millions of people. Imagine the pressure of making America laugh every night. I guess I prefer the weekly sermon.

But why *do* we laugh?

Laughter is one of those interesting aspects of human life that is hard to explain, like hiccups. It is actually pretty funny to hear how scientists attempt to explain laughter:

> Fifteen facial muscles contract and stimulation of the zygomatic major muscle (the main lifting mechanism of your upper lip) occurs. Meanwhile, the respiratory system is upset by the epiglottis half-closing the larynx, so that air intake occurs irregularly, making you gasp. In extreme circumstances, the tear ducts are activated, so that while the mouth is opening and closing and the struggle for oxygen intake continues, the face becomes moist and often red (or purple). The noises that usually accompany this bizarre behavior range from sedate giggles to boisterous guffaws.[4]

I suppose that pretty much sums it up.

Laughter doesn't neatly fit into the evolutionary paradigm; there's no real purpose for it as far as survival or digestion or circulation or any of those types of functions. At the end of the day it's a mysterious human behavior. Biology has a hard time pinning it down.

The psychological study of humor is similar. Psychology's best theory is the "incongruity theory." "The incongruity theory suggests that humor arises when logic and familiarity are replaced by things that don't normally go together. Researcher Thomas Veatch says a joke becomes funny when we expect one outcome and another happens."[5]

That isn't funny. But there is something to it. A joke becomes funny when we expect one thing and then something else entirely comes about. This might help us understand the laughter of the happy church, the giggles and guffaws of the people of God who are in on the unexpected turn.

Laughter emerges when the actual outcome is not the expected outcome. How about the greatest reversal of all time? The whole world was expecting one thing, when . . . surprise! Jesus wins. The tomb is empty. You thought he was dead. He isn't. And we, by faith, are in on it.

Eugene Peterson writes, "Laughter is a result of living in the midst of God's great works." We get to see how God turns evil for good, how God returns exiles to their homeland—how God overcomes death with life. This is not the absence of suffering or the denial of the realities of pain, says Peterson, but

> the joy comes because God knows how to wipe away tears, and, in his resurrection work, create the smile of new life. Joy is what God gives, not what we work up. Laughter is the delight that things are working together for good to those who love God, not the giggles that betray the nervousness of a precarious defense system. The joy that develops in the Christian way of discipleship is an overflow of spirits that comes from feeling good not about yourself but about God.[6]

The expected outcome, the outcome the darkened world expects, is not the actual outcome. Laughter is an expression among the people of God founded on the secret, insider knowledge that God is actually in charge and heaven wins in the end for all who follow in the way of Jesus.

Happy Reversal

As Luke recounts the Sermon on the Plain, Jesus outlined the paradox of the kingdom of God in this way:

Jesus looked at his disciples and said,

"Happy are you poor;
      the Kingdom of God is yours!
"Happy are you who are hungry now;
      you will be filled!
"Happy are you who weep now;
      you will laugh!

"Happy are you when people hate you, reject you, insult you, and say that you are evil, all because of the Son of Man! Be glad when that happens and dance for joy, because a great reward is kept for you in heaven. For their ancestors did the very same things to the prophets." (Luke 6:20-23 GNT)

It's as if Jesus says, "Happy Church! Happy are you! Happy are you poor, for the riches of the kingdom of God are yours to be claimed! Happy are you hungry, for the deep satisfaction of being fed by God himself for all eternity is yours to be claimed! Happy are you who cry, you who are sad! Now you cry. Now you shed tears. Now the pain of this world is too much at times, and you lose yourself in the sadness and the darkness and the tears flow. Now there are moments of deep shadow; days of unshakable doubt and strain and stress. Now you are part of a world that takes away. But be happy, you church! God has grabbed hold of you and lifted you and placed you in his care. God has made you a people of his own keeping. God has set you in the gunnels of his own ship, and the waves of life in this world will never tip it."

Jesus' preaching in the Sermon on the Plain and the Sermon on the Mount (Matthew 5) are often described as great reversals. He seems to turn the whole world on its head.

Humor emerges when the unexpected arrives. When the next thing we expect is replaced by its opposite. Why do we laugh? Because Christ has set up for us a great reversal. The kingdom of God is breaking through in our lives, in our own hearts, and as it breaks through it makes the all the false kingdoms of life look silly—silly enough to laugh at.

The great enemy, the evil boss, the horrific government, the overlord of this world who threatens us, suddenly they all appear as silly as a toddler wearing a plastic crown and yelling, "I'm king! I'm king!" The forces that yesterday terrified us today appear as frightening as a kitten playing a piano. The light of Christ reveals the foolishness of false powers, and the contrast is comical.

> **The kingdom of God is breaking through in our lives, in our own hearts, and as it breaks through it makes the all the false kingdoms of life look silly— silly enough to laugh at.**

How can Jesus proclaim such an unexpected outcome, such a paradoxical reversal? Everything is turned on its head at the cross, where the reversal is engineered.

Jesus' great reversal is won on the cross of Calvary. The cross is the crane, the block and tackle that turns our heaviest downturn into a heavenly victory. Because Jesus descended into the lowest depths, he raises us to the highest heights. But we must follow him through the cross.

The laughter we meet in Jesus is found on the other side of repentance.

Some resolve the paradox "Happy are the sad" this way: When we are sad and mourn our sins in repentance, we will be happy to feel the salvation of Jesus. I'd like to take it a bit deeper than that, but I think it approaches the same point. The reversal is won at the cross where all of our sin is atoned once and for all. Go low in honest repentance and we find the elevation that lifts us heavenward. Take an honest assessment of our sin and its hell-directed trajectory, and in our repentance, mourning and grief we meet the upward lift of the Spirit of God, the Spirit of the risen Christ, lifting us to heaven.

"Humble yourselves before the Lord, and he will exalt you," wrote James (James 4:10). For as Paul declared, "The wages of sin is death, but the free gift of God is eternal life in Christ Jesus our Lord" (Romans 6:23). This is the unexpected outcome. This is the actual outcome overshadowing the expected outcome and breaking in to resolve the tension with joy. This is the basis of the glad spirit of the believer. In Christ we are forgiven.

In Jesus there is a great reversal. The kingdom breaks in just when we think darkness has won. And we laugh. We laugh in the face of evil. Laughter is an emblem of Christ's victory over sin and death. Laughter is a promise and a hope. It's a sign of a coming kingdom.

Jump the Waves

C. S. Lewis wrote an imaginative book called *The Screwtape Letters*, in which a demon named Wormwood is tasked with preventing a man from turning to Jesus. Wormwood's assignment is to keep the man deceived and to keep him from seeing the truth.

His Uncle Screwtape, a much more advanced demon, sends Wormwood letters of advice—effective tactics for keeping a soul from Christ. One of his tactics is to keep this guy miserable. To keep him far from true joy. To keep twisting and perverting the things around him, finding ways to diminish his pleasures while increasing his desires for ungodly things. This is going to be hard, his uncle explains, because God (their enemy) is "a hedonist at heart. . . . He has filled His world full of pleasures."

There's nothing so frustrating to the demons but that God is happy by nature and never ceases shamelessly pouring out blessings and goodness. So, the uncle demon instructs Wormwood to keep his victim frozen like a child on the beach, afraid to go into the waters. Keep him on the shores, afraid of the sea foam and bubbles, because if the man actually ventures out into the sea of God he will find that "out in His sea, there is pleasure, and more pleasure. He makes no secret of it; at His right hand are 'pleasures for evermore' [Psalm 16:11]."[7] Awful pleasures!

To get into the sea we have to jump the waves. The trouble is, the waves keep coming. They never stop. The devil wants to keep us on the shore, stultified in fear of the foam. We must steel our heart and take courage to leap through the foam to the sea of pleasures evermore.

Jump the waves.

The only really decent scar I have on my body is from surfing. As a boy from Colorado, I grew up visiting my grandparents in Jacksonville, Florida. For one or two weeks each summer, I had to prove myself to be a surfer. All the boys my age rode their bikes from their beach houses every morning with surfboards under their arms. I could ski, but the first time I tried to ride a bike with a surfboard under my arm, I almost hit the mailbox at the end of the driveway and wound up flat on my back in the grass. But still I resolved to try.

Pushing against those waves with a surfboard is hard work, and I could never get myself out far enough. So, I'd try to ride the second little break in the waves near the beach. One day, too close to shore, I had only pulled myself halfway up onto the board when the nose planted itself in the sand and the back of the board planted itself in my leg. I proved I was a Colorado boy after all. Although I did look pretty cool carrying my board out of the ocean with blood dripping down my leg. I acted like it was a shark bite.

Evil powers are intent on keeping us in the rip and pull of the waves, right at the edge of shore. They don't want us to experience the deep and abiding peace of God's ocean of joy. No, they want us to struggle. Battered and wearied. Desperate and breathless. Doubtful that peace and joy even exist out past the white foam and froth. But if we jump the waves, we will enter the sea of God's true pleasures. All we need is a little elevation.

Laughter is a jump over the waves, a leap from finitude to infinity. The grasp of infinity is almost imperceptible in the life of a Christian. Our external reality is just as bad as everyone else's, but inside us there is God's infinite life—and we laugh.

Laughing with Friends

There is the happy Christian, and there is the happy church. If we are truly going to pursue happiness, if we are going to follow the vein of Christians from every age and pursue happiness by knowing God and being used for his purposes, we are not going to do it alone. We get to do it with friends.

Laughter is done among friends. It's contagious. Charles Dickens, who so valued laughter that he made it the key feature of the conversion of Ebenezer Scrooge in *The Christmas Carol*, once wrote, "It is a fair, even handed, noble adjustment of things that, while there is infection in disease and sorrow, there is nothing in the world so irresistibly contagious as laughter and good humor."[8] Dickens understood that when we see someone laugh, we can't help but laugh with them. As Richard Foster writes, "Laughter begets laughter. It is one of those few things we multiply by giving."[9]

In my youth group years ago we used to play a game called the laughing train. One person lies down on his or her back. The next person lies down with his or her head on the first person's stomach. You continue stacking people like that, one after the other, head to tummy. Then someone starts to laugh. And it's so silly, the head bouncing on a laughing tummy, that everyone erupts into laughter at once and the room starts to shake with laughter.

Sometimes we laugh alone, but the best laughter is shared with friends.

The happy church laughs.

But we Christians forget to laugh! Have you ever met a Christian who forgot to laugh? Could it be, just maybe, that we are taking ourselves too seriously?

British apologist G. K. Chesterton was a master of laughter, puns and one-liners. We might think it was just a product of his nature. Some are given easily to laughter and mirth. Others have melancholy spirits; their biology keeps them sullen and solemn. Like the cool, Nordic blood and long winters of Garrison Keillor's Minnesota Lutheran community on Lake Woebegone, laughter doesn't come easy for them. Some are given to laughter, others to be somber. But Chesterton didn't see it that way. For him, it was a Christian duty to laugh, a serious business in fact, hanging in the balance between heaven and hell: "Solemnity flows out of men naturally; but laughter is a leap. It is easy to be heavy: hard to be light. Satan fell by the force of gravity."[10]

Philosopher Søren Kierkegaard illustrated the model of Christian faith, the "knight of faith," as a man with elevation, a man who could feel the lightness of eternity right in the middle of the regular and ordinary vicissitudes of everyday life: "Most people live completely absorbed in worldly joys and sorrows; they are benchwarmers who do not take part in the dance. The knights of infinity are ballet dancers and have elevation."[11] Laughter is elevation. We are too much overcome by the sullenness of this despairing world, when "by my God I can leap over a wall" (Psalm 18:29). When we laugh, we take a leap.

Our willingness to laugh together makes room for glimpses of the kingdom. In high school I became a volunteer leader for a youth ministry. My very first act as a volunteer was to dress up as a cowboy in a skit about going to the dentist. Come to think of it, that may be my first official act of ministry. We laughed. It broke the ice. Later, we could sing and talk seriously about Jesus.

We forget to laugh sometimes. We are so serious, so dour. Have you forgotten? Christ is victorious! Have you not heard? Christ has won! The kingdom is emerging.

You Shall Laugh

Jesus talked about laughter: "Blessed are you who weep now, for you shall laugh!" (Luke 6:21). *You shall laugh*, says Jesus. This *will* happen. You will know that you are in heaven—you will know that heaven is in you—when you laugh. Laughter is a marker of the heavenly, a characteristic of life eternal. Laughter is a value to Jesus. It's an emblem of his victory over this world.

I wish we had a verse that said "Jesus laughed." It would be nice to balance out "Jesus wept" (John 11:35)—universally celebrated as the easiest verse to memorize. The closest we get is Luke 10:21, where Jesus "rejoiced in the Holy Spirit," presumably in some way that was visible to the eyewitnesses who later recorded it. For some reason we don't see Jesus laugh in the Gospels.

Chesterton ended his great work *Orthodoxy* with the statement that despite all that was revealed by the incarnation of Jesus, God had still hidden something of his character, something so profound that to reveal it to us would crush us. There was something still hidden so weighty we couldn't take it. He said, "I have sometimes fancied that it was his mirth."[12]

Maybe we don't get to see God's sense of humor because it's so immense and glorious we would not survive its revelation. But even if we don't have a verse that says "Jesus laughed," we know he did. Laughter is part of the human experience.

The more I think about the ascension, the moment when Jesus rose bodily into heaven, the more I think he was laughing all the way. For all its theological significance, this is a genuinely comical moment. Jesus must have had a twinkle in his eye when he told the disciples "I'll be with you forever to the end of time" as he was literally leaving them, disappearing into the sky.

So there the disciples stand, on the Mount of Olives, staring with their mouths hanging open. They watch as Jesus bodily ascends into the sky and disappears behind a cloud. Now *that's* something to see. As they are peering into the sky, two angels appear (Acts 1:11) and ask, "What are you looking at?"

"What are we looking at? Our best friend just launched himself from the ground all the way behind that cloud!"

I can almost hear Jesus laughing from heaven.

When I say this is comical, I do not mean to be irreverent. I mean it is rooted in paradox. Jesus proclaims himself both present and absent. I'm with you, and I'm gone. This isn't a genuine paradox, actually, because it will be resolved by the presence of the Holy Spirit. In the end it makes sense. We know that now, and so we can appreciate the humor. Humor emerges from the presence of two opposing facts creating a tension that is suddenly resolved. The expected outcome (Jesus' absence) becomes the very occasion for the actual outcome (Jesus' presence by his Holy Spirit). Don't let anyone tell you God is without a sense of humor.

Laughter is a value to Jesus. Laughter and heaven are constant companions; they almost always appear together. Heaven is the ultimate resolution of tension. Life ends in death. Life and death are opposing facts. But then, in walks heaven.

Why is there laughter in a happy church? Because laughter is an emblem of the victory of Christ over the shadows of this present darkness. When we laugh, we show we are wearing the colors of the coming kingdom; waving the banner of the victorious King and the eternal life he has won for us.

Laughter is an emblem of the victory of Christ over the shadows of this present darkness.

God made the tomb laugh to expel his lifeless Son. With an exuberant "Ha!" the universe itself was made to laugh at the claims of death, and the Spirit ranged all creation with the roaring laughter of the risen Lord in the jubilation of life eternal.

Laugh, Christian. God has won!

7

The People of Limitless Hope

And there are truths, whether we know them
or not, which must be believed if we would attain
to a happy life, that is, to eternal life.

Augustine of Hippo

• • •

I have never been good at faking a positive attitude.

One summer during college I was a knife salesman. I performed in-home product demonstrations by referral and then tried to close the deal. The manager did his best to teach us to maintain a positive attitude—"Believe it and achieve it!" He taught us to make signs for ourselves with markers on construction paper and place them on the floor next to our beds. The idea was that when we got out of bed we would see these signs and be encouraged. I tried this. I wrote: "You're going to sell a Chefmaker today!" (the biggest, most expensive set of knives). But I could never fool myself. I'd wake up, look down at the sign—"You're going to sell a Chefmaker today!"— but before I could stop myself, I'd think, *Nah, you're not. You've only sold two of those all summer—and those were to relatives.*

Jesus doesn't need a fake positive attitude from us. Yes, there's something to training our minds to look on the bright side now and then, but Jesus doesn't demand fake belief. He wants us to have a solid, core conviction that his promises are true.

Jesus doesn't demand fake belief. He wants us to have a solid, core conviction that his promises are true.

They say our attitude is 10 percent what happens to us and 90 percent how we react to it. Who calculates these percentages? I guess it seems reasonable. The way we react to things comes from our core belief system. We run what happens to us through the paradigms of our core beliefs—and react.

Can we believe there is reason to be happy in the Lord? Is there something in our core belief system that will enable us to be truly happy in the Lord, even in the face of the worst and most painful experiences?

Ultimately, in our search for a foundation for happiness, it comes down to one thing: the empty tomb.

Christians are challenged by others for their optimism and belief in heaven. Non-Christians see this as a weakness. "Christians *need* to believe in life after death. They can't come to terms with the reality that life snuffs out when the body runs out of steam. Psychologically, they need something to keep them going, so they drum up a theory of life after death to make them feel better. Pie in the sky in the great by and by."

That is not what we get in Scripture. Don't succumb to the notion of Christianity as a false hope. Push hard, question hard and drive hard into the Scriptures. I encourage you to dig deep into your convictions, your theology, the way you think about God, life and the world. Push and dig down to the bedrock, and you will find that there is good reason to be happy in the Lord.

We are not talking about self-deception here. Professor Ellen Charry writes, "Happiness is not a matter of manipulating the world to secure our desire, but taking pleasure in being who Scripture teaches we are. Happiness is living with theological integrity."[1]

We are not talking about groundless attitude adjustment or positive thinking by sheer willpower. We are talking about finding something real to hang our faith on. Something solid enough to dismiss doubt and give us the strength to move into the conviction that God is real, his promises are true, and we can believe in him. And we have one thing to look at, one thing we can always return to, one thing that is a solid fact: the tomb in which Jesus of Nazareth was laid is empty.

The empty tomb is the linchpin of the gospel for Paul. He told the Corinthian church that without the empty tomb, without the resurrection, there is nothing: "If Christ has not been raised, your faith is futile and you are still in your sins. Then those also who have fallen asleep in Christ have perished. If in Christ we have hope in this life only, we are of all people most to be pitied" (1 Corinthians 15:17-19). If Christ is not raised, we are still lost in our sins. If Christ is not raised, we are most to be pitied because we are the fools who staked our lives on a false promise.

As New Testament scholar Richard Hays says,

> For Paul, the whole web of Christian discourse is airy nonsense if it is not anchored in the truth of the resurrection of Jesus. Christian preaching becomes a system of delusions, offering nothing but lies and empty gestures. The gospel has no power to save us if Christ is not raised.[2]

It is airy nonsense, lies and empty gestures. All of Christianity is a fairy tale, a foolish myth, an airy fantasy if Jesus Christ did not rise bodily from the dead. Why does Paul say this?

Belief in the resurrection is a pretty tall order. If we arranged in order all the hard things we have to believe to be Christian, Jesus rising from the dead would be one of the hardest. Let's start by believing God is real, that God is good or that creation is beautiful because God made it. Let's sit there for a while, and then we might start trusting the Bible more—especially when it seems to enhance our marriage or helps us succeed at work or as parents. But resurrection?

If we are to be the happy people of God, the happy church Psalms talks about, the blessed and happy people Jesus claims in the Sermon on the Mount, then we need a foundation for our faith. We need something firm to stand on at the core of our convictions and at the center of our theological integrity.

God gave it to us in the resurrection of Jesus from the dead.

The most hardened and cynical historians still cannot come to terms with this phenomenon. Yes, they might be able to produce alternative theories about where the body of Jesus of Nazareth ended up, but these never stand up to the incontrovertible reality that within months of the event thousands of people believed Jesus was raised from the dead—and believed it with conviction. They believed it with such conviction they staked their lives on it and were even tortured and killed on its account. This is the thing that even the most cynical scholars can't dismiss. How do they explain such widespread, convictional, high-stakes commitment to the empty tomb and risen body of Jesus if it didn't actually happen?

They can't.

The tomb is empty. Jesus is alive. And that changes everything.

The Cross and What Comes After

One year, I taught the Heidelberg Catechism on Wednesday nights at church. I think everyone in the class was surprised at how relevant it felt to think through these deep issues of Christian theology, to dig down to core convictions and to study the way we think about God and life and the world. In commenting on the Heidelberg Catechism, Kevin DeYoung writes,

The best news about Jesus is that through Him we are forgiven our sins, set free from the law, made right with God, and can stand confident before our Creator. All this is announced to us in the *gospel*. The gospel is not a summons to kingdom living or a message about what we can do for God or a description of our efforts at cultural transformation. The gospel, according to Paul's summary in 1 Corinthians 15, is the good news that Jesus Christ died for our sins and rose again on the third day.[3]

Jesus' death on the cross paid for our sins. That's the heart of the good news. The wrath of God is satisfied, and we come back to the zero sum, where we no longer owe God for our sins. Jesus, in his atoning sacrifice on the cross, has paid to overcome that division and bridge the separation between humans and God by making us righteous again before the Father by paying the debt on our behalf.

What then? Is that all? If the gospel is merely the news that God paid off our debt in Jesus' death on the cross, well, we might feel relieved but not really *happy*.

But there is more: the resurrection of Jesus from the dead. The empty tomb tells us God is not finished with us when we reach the sum of zero. God intends life and blessing, *eternal* life and *eternal* blessing. God intends all things to be set right, all pain to be ended, all suffering to cease and all death to be swallowed up in life. Happiness is believing this is true.

In Jesus we are promised an afterlife of great glory. Jesus is the firstborn risen from the dead (Colossians 1:18). *Firstborn* means there are many to follow. You and I, in Christ, are promised heaven.

You can take *this* life; I have a life *to come*.

Paul wrote to the Philippian church while he was imprisoned in Rome waiting to be tried by the courts of the emperor for inciting disruptive gatherings around the Roman Empire. He said to them,

"One thing I do: forgetting what lies behind and straining forward to what lies ahead, I press on toward the goal for the prize of the upward call of God in Christ Jesus" (Philippians 3:13-14).

Paul knew he was waiting to face authorities who could take his life, and they eventually did. He was beheaded (most likely) by decree of Emperor Nero. He knew all that was a possibility, but still he writes of pressing forward. The upward call lies ahead. As if to say, "You can kill me, Nero, but you can't kill me!"

So we all likewise overcome. You can kill me, cancer, but you can't kill me. You can take my life, you broken and evil world, but I've got a secret of great joy. I am eternal because of Jesus.

An eternal life has been won for us by Jesus on the cross. An upward call awaits us.

Our Then Defines Our Now

It matters that our future is secure eternally in Jesus. It matters a lot. It shapes our life differently. It matters not only for our place in eternity but also for our life right now. Where we are headed after death changes how we live here and now.

Imagine two forced laborers.[4] Each is put to work by his master doing the same menial, boring, soul-sucking job, hour after hour, day in and day out. One is given a contract: "After this year, I'll set you free with $20 in your pocket for bus fare." The other is told, "After one year of this work, I will give you a million dollars and restore you to your family." Which one will whistle while he works? You see, the future matters to the present.

Then alters *now*. So let it. Connect with the promises Christ gives you. This is what Peter calls the imperishable, undefiled and unfading inheritance kept in heaven for you (1 Peter 1:4). Are you letting that future shape your present?

Because of the *then*, we live differently in the *now*. Paul wrote, "I press on toward the goal for the prize of the upward call of God in

Christ Jesus" (Philippians 3:14). "I press on." That's right now. The present. The promises of Christ are not merely to deal with the past. The promises of Christ are not only to a future hope of a heavenly home. The promises of Christ are for *right now*. Connecting with him and living for him today in the joy of the surpassing worth of knowing Jesus Christ right now, I press on.

"My business has failed and my savings are diminishing with every passing day, but I press on."

"My marriage is damaged severely and life with my husband is like walking on a bad hip, but I press on."

"My children are troubled and disobedient, my father is dying of cancer, my dearest love is lying on the operating table, and I'm wondering when the bleeding will stop, but I press on."

Why? Because despite whatever today holds, the future is good. Jesus has guaranteed it.

In American history we can look quickly to the legacy of the African American spirituals. People unjustly enslaved sang boldly of the freedom they knew in Christ and the future hope of a world beyond this world. At the same time they were lending relief and enabling escape, these visions of future hope served to alter the present order. Not only did they give the oppressed a song to sing, but they fed flames of defiant resistance. Whenever we sing *Deep River* or *Swing Low, Sweet Chariot*, we remember how powerful a song of the future—a song of hope—can be.

Placing hope in the coming world on the basis of the promises of Christ is not to abandon the present world or give up on needed change. In fact, being the community of limitless hope often means finding the energy to shape the present by our future vision. C. S. Lewis wrote,

> If you read history you will find that the Christians who did
> most for the present world were just those who thought most

of the next. The Apostles themselves, who set on foot the conversion of the Roman Empire, the great men who built up the Middle Ages, the English Evangelicals who abolished the Slave Trade, all left their mark on Earth, precisely because their minds were occupied with Heaven. It is since Christians have largely ceased to think of the other world that they have become so ineffective in this.[5]

It seems we've lost a little heaven hope in our churches. We seem embarrassed by it. The hope of heaven is sometimes the only power available to aid our persistent pursuit of joy.

The past is behind me. Whatever was good was to the glory of Christ, and whatever bad is covered by his grace and righteousness. The future is before me. However many days I still have on earth I will receive as a gift, but I fret not their number, for my inheritance is eternal in the heavens with God. Today, now, in this moment, I press on. That's the power of the hope of glory in me.

Ann Voskamp writes in *One Thousand Gifts*,

> Though my marriage tree may not bud and though my crop of children may fail and my work produce little yield, though there is no money in the bank and no dream left in the heart, though others may choose different ways to live their one life, till my last heaving breath, I will fight to the death for this: "I will take joy" (Habakkuk 3:18).[6]

If you belong to Christ, there is an upward call in your life. An upward call that dismisses the broken past, promises a glorified future and totally alters the present. Take joy. Give thanks for the upward call of Jesus Christ! You belong to heaven.

A Heaven Community on an Earthly Mission

The contingencies of the present moment do not define the limits of our joy. Hope extends our soul beyond the present tense into the future. The happy church is a community sure of its expectation, certain of what is promised. We are a people certain that death has no hold on us. We live now in the full knowledge that our souls are held in an eternal stronghold, and nothing can change that. We are a community of eternals in a world of death.

But we get stuck looking at the things that bog us down here and now and believing we belong to them, that they own us. But they don't own us. Christ owns us. *Now* and *then*.

> **We are a people certain that death has no hold on us. We live now in the full knowledge that our souls are held in an eternal stronghold, and nothing can change that.**

Dietrich Bonhoeffer's last words are reported to have been, "This is the end—for me, the beginning of life."[7] In his last letter to his fiancée, written from prison four months before his execution, he wrote, "You must not think that I am unhappy. What is happiness and unhappiness? It depends so little on circumstances; it depends really only on that which happens inside a person."[8] Inside Dietrich Bonhoeffer was hope, confidence in a future life with Christ that the end of his natural life could not shake. But it wasn't his alone. It was his in the community of faith.

I know your church is in touch with this faith. I know your church knows this hope. Has it been misplaced in plain sight?

It seems an odd suggestion but it's one I make from time to time. You should go to a funeral. You should attend a memorial service in your church. One for somebody you hardly knew. We say things in those services that we don't say much on Sunday mornings. It's for good reason Ecclesiastes teaches,

> It is better to go to the house of mourning
>   than to go to the house of feasting,

for this is the end of all mankind,
  and the living will lay it to heart. (Ecclesiastes 7:2)

Sometimes, it is better to go to a funeral than a birthday party. At the funeral we rehearse the deep truths too often forgotten, that our life is held by Christ past death. The birthday party can be a little happier when the celebrant knows she is not one more year closer to the eternal abyss but nearer to eternal life in her Lord! Your church knows this.

The entire process of aging and death has been isolated and sanitized in our culture, to the detriment of our spiritual health. The same Bible I hold in my hands to preach on Sunday has likely been sitting on the end of a hospital bed that week. The church misplaces its foundation for hope when it isolates itself from the darkness where hope shines brightest.

Hope is a leap past death, an assurance of life eternal.

My friend Steve Hayner passed away this year. I call him my friend not to make some claim of self-importance but because he granted me friendship openly and freely on no merits of my own. He had no business being my friend, to be honest. He the seminary president, me the unknown suburban pastor. His kindness in friendship was a grace. That's why I claim it, along with just about anyone who ever knew him.

Losing him to pancreatic cancer was a deep tragedy for us all. Steve was one of the most joyful men I have ever met. The day he passed, I had a realization: "I want to learn to smile like Steve Hayner."

Steve knew hope beyond death.

As he was able through declining health, he wrote blog posts on the CaringBridge website. InterVarsity Press has compiled those posts, along with his wife Sharol's posts and further thoughts, into a beautiful book, *Joy in the Journey*. It is a monument to hope and joy in the face of earthly death. Steve wrote one day early in his diagnosis,

All life on planet earth is terminal, and while we can certainly contribute to our own well-being in amazing ways, none of us is ultimately in control. One day, my life will be swallowed up by Life. And for today, I am choosing truth, joy and love wherever and however I can. I am resolute in my desire to learn, to fulfill my calling and to engage each day with as much joy as I am graciously given or can borrow.[9]

Not one of us is getting out of here alive. But, then again, not one of us will taste ultimate death either. How do we cultivate the community of limitless hope? If my joy runs out, maybe there is some I can borrow.

Even when we feel stuck, we are not stuck. We belong to another order of life—a life won for us by Jesus Christ. Because of this belonging, we can even live with gratitude through hardship and in disappointment. Because of Christ, we belong to another order of life not measured by how things are going here. Paul's hope was founded in this: "Our citizenship is in heaven, and from it we await a Savior, the Lord Jesus Christ" (Philippians 3:20).

Our hope is sourced in something eternal. Hope like that cannot run out. We are the society of limitless hope.

The Morning Star

Revelation is a book about the end of the world. But it's also a picture of the beginning. The end of this world is just the beginning.

We have now in this world a universe created by God and loaned to imperfect men and women. We inhabit the world we have shaped. All its brokenness is our brokenness. All its hopelessness is ours to own.

But in Revelation we see the world to come, the city built by God coming down to restore all things. We see the world created by God and taken again into his holy hands. Restored. Reconciled.

Renewed. Redeemed. So we have hope. Revelation is a letter of hope written by the Spirit of God to renew churches suffering deeply, to inspire Christians who were in horrible depression, wondering if there could be another reality than what they were experiencing just then. It was written to remind them, and to remind us, of the morning star: Jesus.

Why is Jesus called the morning star?

The morning star is the planet Venus. It shines bright early in the east, as the sky brightens and all the other stars fade out. It is a precursor, a forerunner. When we watch the morning star and wait, soon we find ourself with the full light and warmth of the sun on our face.

Jesus has gone before us into the coming kingdom. If we look first to him, all these things will follow.

Jesus is the morning star. Jesus is the rising sun. Turning our faces toward Jesus fills our hearts with hope.

I venture to guess you do not suffer persecution like in the early church. Certainly, I don't. We are not threatened as we gather like our friends who are worshiping today in secret in China or Afghanistan. We don't fear the authorities like our friends in Egypt. Still we thirst. Still we hurt. We long for wholeness in our lives; we long for the night to end and the morning to come.

"'Come.' And let the one who is thirsty come; let the one who desires take the water of life without price" (Revelation 22:17). The wholeness we want is exactly what we see in Revelation. We see the city of God, made by his own hand, where there is no more death, no more violence, no more uncleanness, no more pollution of body, mind, spirit and soul. All is set right, as God intends.

The hope we have in Jesus is that this world is coming. This is how it all ends and how it all begins again. A time is coming when all judgments will be conferred. "Behold, I am coming soon, bringing my recompense with me, to repay each one for what he has done" (Revelation 22:12).

Judgment day is coming. You know what that means!

First, it means nobody is going to "get away with it." Imagine you are one of the twenty-seven million people in slavery today. Most of them are stuck under overlords who claim they owe them vast sums of money, so much that they could never pay, and so they are worked to death in their debt. Judgment day means that unjust overlord is not going to get away with it. He will answer to God.

Second, it means all will be set right. The city of God is coming, where we will walk in the presence of the Lord and see his face. All our longings and all our thirsts will be satisfied.

Sometimes I imagine trying to make it through life believing this world is all there is. I don't know how a marriage, for one thing, can survive that. If we think this world is all there is, and that one day our life will blink out and everything we did will be forever forgotten, then the first time our spouse disappoints us (and he or she *will*), we will immediately head for the door thinking, *I only have a few years to be happy!* But this view is not true. All our desires, all our unmet needs, all the deepest longings in our heart to be loved, to be significant, to have a life that means something—those longings and thirsts will finally come home to the city of God where they will, for the first time and forever, be fully satisfied as we drink our fill from the water of life.

We need this hope. What we believe about the future changes everything about our present. What we believe will happen in the end changes the whole game. We need to grasp the reality of the hope found in the morning star, Jesus. The church remembers together, hopes together and feels the joy of the morning sun at the break of day.

It is not an empty promise, an opiate to get us to accept life as we know it. It's a contract. It's guaranteed by the empty tomb and sealed by the Holy Spirit on our heart. This is happening in the end: we will drink from the water of life, without price, and will never be thirsty again.

How can we—a rational people who have already learned to swallow the bitter sours of disappointment—experience such hope? Because Jesus paid the price on our behalf, we get this hope, we receive a foretaste of the eternally satisfying draught of the water of life when we believe in Jesus, his life, his crucifixion and his resurrection.

What we believe about the future changes everything about our present. What we believe will happen in the end changes the whole game.

We remind one another of this in the community of hope. We pursue radical joy as the people of God when we reenact these truths for one another.

In our church lobby is a memorial board. Every member of our church who has passed away since our founding in 1972 has a nameplate. How does your church remember? Those gone from us are not gone forever. Those absent from us are not lost; they have only gone before us into the eternal places prepared. "Our hope is built on nothing less / than Jesus' blood and righteousness."[10] Together we look to him and trust, we place our faith in Jesus the morning star, whose light foretells a whole world coming in light. Believing in him is the beginning of hope.

Yes, I Will Do It

Pastor Steven Vryhof was traveling through Sweden when he stopped at church in a small village on the coast.[11] State-run Lutheranism isn't exactly thriving, and there were only fourteen people there for church.

The priest was a "slender blonde lad" fresh out of seminary. Worship was a rather rote episode of Lutheran hymns, a sung liturgy and the standard motions of Communion. As the priest was putting the Communion elements away, a woman came down the aisle rolling her mother in a wheelchair. She was coming for Communion too. Her look was vacant and her head slumped over. Her mouth hung open and she was a drooling; it was an awkward moment.

The young minister looked at the old woman, fed her the bread and the wine, and recited these words—words that suddenly rang in Steven's ears as the most important words spoken from one human being to another—"Our Lord Jesus Christ, whose body and blood you have received, preserve your soul unto everlasting life."

Then something coincidental happened, if you believe in coincidence. That precise moment the bells of the church started pealing, "ringing and resonating and resounding and reverberating through the church and through me," Vryhof said, "making the hair on the back of my head stand up. Heaven touched earth and it seemed very much that *Our Lord Jesus Christ* himself was saying: *Yes, I will do that!*"

Christian happiness is sometimes a delayed happiness. We recognize that as long as we are in this world, there will be suffering. But even so, we are happy because we know for certain Christ will set things right. God will bring the victory. It is already begun. The tomb is empty, and that ever stands as testimony. Jesus has said, God has declared, "Yes. I will do that."

What happens when the church lives with a hope like that? The happy church happens.

Imagine a community that gathers weekly for an hour in a tone of hope, using only hope language in full confidence that Jesus will fulfill his promises. Imagine a community that bars all talk of limitations and shortfalls and things that cannot come to pass. Imagine that it only speaks of the limitless resources of their Creator and acts on the shared belief that anything can happen because God is in control and God's power is fathomless.

Jesus ended his time on earth with a vision of great hope. The final words of Jesus in the Bible occur in Revelation: "I, Jesus, have sent my angel to testify to you about these things for the churches. I am the root and the descendant of David, the bright morning star. . . . Surely I am coming soon" (Revelation 22:16, 20).

We have hope. A hope not of this world. A hope that is not empty optimism. A hope that is founded in a person, God: the Alpha and the Omega, the Beginning and the End. A hope founded in Jesus. This can get us through.

Imagine a "hope community" like that resting in the confidence that all will be well in the end, and the ordinary vicissitudes of the day are fleeting in comparison to the eternal horizons ahead. In a community of such hope, the phrase "It can't be done" becomes "We'll find a way—the Lord will do it."

What if there were a community like that?

Executives pay thousands of dollars to enroll their senior leaders in retreats to increase optimism and harmony. What if every church in North America promoted the same spirit? This is the happy church, and enrollment is totally free! (Although watch out for a few expenses on the back end. Some say it will actually cost us everything.)

This is the people whose God is the Lord. This is the true community of limitless hope, the people who live the promises of God. Their future is certain. Nothing is impossible for them. Their hope is not in their own potential or in their ability to stay optimistic. Their hope is in the Lord their God, who has never failed.

The tomb is empty, and the promises are guaranteed. The future we have in God is without bounds. That is why we hope. That is why we're happy.

The tomb is empty, and the promises are guaranteed. The future we have in God is without bounds.

Suffering the Mission of Joy

*If you ask people who don't believe in God
why they don't, the number one reason will be suffering.
If you ask people who believe in God when they grew the most
spiritually, the number one answer will be suffering.*

JOHN ORTBERG

• • •

I'm sorry, David. I really am."

A friend had asked me to coffee. He was a pastor like me, but he was in his second career. His first business took off, and he sold it. His second business sold in less than four years, and when he was working up the details on the third with some investors and friends, he felt the call to ministry. Stepping away from salaries counted in "figures," he answered the call to Christ in a new direction.

Now he was in a small and dying church. The turnaround was just not taking hold. He was frustrated, and key leaders were placing the blame on him.

"That hurts. It really does, I know. I bet you wish you could go back to the business world."

He looked up at me sharply.

"Wait a minute, Tim. I'm frustrated, but I'm the happiest I've ever been in my life. I don't think you first-career church guys get it. There is nothing like knowing every single thing I do matters for Jesus."

Every single thing you do can matter for Jesus. You don't even have to become a pastor or a missionary to pull that off! It takes total submission to Jesus wherever you sit. And when everything you do matters to Jesus, when your life is an answer to his call, there is happiness deep and wide.

The Mission to Bring Joy to the World

We are sent into the world on a mission of joy. Remember, it's called the *good* news: we declare good news. Our mission is to bring this good news to the world, to bring joy to the world in the name of Jesus. In this mission, suffering will come to us and we will go to suffering. Suffering will come to us as the world rejects and opposes the light of Christ. We will go to suffering as our hearts break with what breaks the heart of God. As a people in pursuit of radical joy, we will be joined to the name and character of Jesus—a man of sorrows familiar with suffering—as we patiently and lovingly receive the world's rejection and graciously take up the burdens of the world's pains. In the midst of that suffering we will yet know joy. We will yet shine like lights.

This is the greatest paradox of all: to gain we have to lose. "Whoever seeks to preserve his life will lose it, but whoever loses his life will keep it" (Luke 17:33). When we lose our life entirely into the purposes of Jesus, we gain eternal life. Happiness comes from perfect submission to Christ, from selfless sacrifice to gladly suffer the mission of joy.

But what if it hurts? What if there is suffering involved in taking up the mission of Jesus?

Yes, there will be suffering. That much is guaranteed. The

church lies at a radically countercultural angle to the common way of life in this world, and so it rubs against the world at every movement. The church and the world move in different trajectories, producing friction and conflict. It hurts to be the church, but there is deep happiness for those who, in humble obedience, take up the mission of joy.

Jesus acknowledged the reality of suffering. On his way to Jerusalem to face his own passion and crucifixion, he took great pains to explain to those

It hurts to be the church, but there is deep happiness for those who, in humble obedience, take up the mission of joy.

with him that suffering is coming for his followers. *Oh yes, you will endure suffering:* "I have said all these things to you to keep you from falling away. They will put you out of the synagogues. Indeed, the hour is coming when whoever kills you will think he is offering service to God" (John 16:1-2). And "Truly, truly, I say to you, you will weep and lament, but the world will rejoice" (John 16:20).

Jesus was never shy about explaining the coming pains of the followers of Christ. We will shed tears. We will be sorrowful—but (can you believe this now?) our sorrow will turn into joy. That's the rest of the verse: "Truly, truly, I say to you, you will weep and lament, but the world will rejoice. You will be sorrowful, but your sorrow will turn into joy" (John 16:20).

It is very difficult when we are in dark places to believe sorrow can turn into joy. Maybe there's nothing in us that believes it. There's no way to compute this in our own minds, and it doesn't fit our own experience. It doesn't make rational sense to us in any way, but Jesus says it. He says it. That might be the only thing we have to hold on to sometimes—*I believe it because Jesus says it; my sorrow will turn into joy.*

This type of joy, this type of *happy*, can't be taken away. If God has established joy in the midst of sorrow, who will be able to tear it down? If the joy we have is God's making, who or what could possibly destroy it?

Jesus says, "I will see you again, and your hearts will rejoice, and no one will take your joy from you" (John 16:22). Yes, in this world we will have trouble, but there is also joy that can't be taken from us—right in the middle of the pain.

The happy church is aware of life's pain in this world. Augustine wrote, "Though human life is compelled to be miserable by all the great evils of this world, it is happy in the hope of the world to come, and in the hope of salvation."[1] There are great evils in this world compelling us to be miserable. But the life centered in Christ is still happy.

John Piper put it another way: "The Calvary road with Jesus is not a joyless road. It is a painful one, but it is a profoundly happy one."[2] The happy people of God are not surprised that there is pain in this life, that there is struggle or that life is full of sickness, disappointment and anxiety, and ends with physical death. The people of God know this. But the deep foundations for happiness in Christ are enough to carry us through, and, more important, they are enough to help us keep believing God is good even as we walk the burdensome road of suffering in his name. The greatest surprise is when we feel the Lord's own joy on the suffering road, and it does not come to us as a product of the environment, it does not spring from the glad and happy surrounds—it comes directly from the hand of God.

The Church of Joyful Obedience

Hannah Whitall Smith published *The Christian's Secret of a Happy Life* in 1870. The secret is obedience. Joyful obedience to Jesus Christ, she said, is the secret of a happy life. Not dutiful obedience. Not puritanical, externally motivated, guilt-driven obedience but *joyful* obedience.

What is joyful obedience? It's when God moves into our desires by his Spirit "to get possession of the inside of us, to take the control and management of our will, and to work it for us." Smith continues, "Then obedience is easy and a delight, and service becomes perfect freedom, until the Christian is forced to explain, 'This happy service! Who could dream earth had such liberty?'"[3]

Joyful submission to the will of God for us becomes a perfect freedom of happy service to Christ. Can the church breed the same attitude in community? Can the church, as a community, as a people pursuing radical joy, take up joyful obedience together? We need to reduplicate the personal experience of joyful obedience for the community of faith together.

Study after study emerge to report that individuals consider themselves happier when their lives are marked with meaning and selfless service to others or to a purpose higher than themselves. One study calls this type of happiness "eudaimonic happiness" (from the Greek word for "blessing") in contrast to immediate pleasure-seeking or "hedonic happiness."[4] This debate is nothing new. In the ancient world, philosophies competed to promote the path to happiness and peace. Stoics subscribed to apathy, teaching that the happy life is curbed against extremes of pleasure and pain. Epicureans disagreed. There must be joyful celebration of good pleasures to increase happiness, they said, to balance out the times of pain. But even they warned against shortsighted hedonism, teaching their followers to live with purpose and meaning among their family and country. The well-lived life would be measured from beginning to end, not at one or two spikes of immediate pleasure.

In every chapter the history of humanity recounts that the happy life is lived with meaning and purpose. The same is true for the church. The church opens up to happiness when it knows its purpose and mission. It can even endure suffering when it knows why—when it knows it is suffering for Jesus.

Author and pastor Don Everts encourages the church to see itself on mission for Christ, promoting a vision of the thriving church:

> And when God's church is thriving, his people are also being sent. As we've seen throughout this book [*Go and Do: Becoming a Missional Christian*], God not only saves and grows and nurtures Christians, he also invites us to get caught up with what he is doing in the world. In this way the church becomes an outpost.... God's work is channeled through and anchored in thriving churches.[5]

The church is God's movement to reach the lost of our community, nation and world with the good news of the gospel of Jesus Christ. When the church is aligned, together and on mission, the exuberance is overwhelming. Pastor Bill Hybels writes,

> There is nothing like the local church when it's working right. Its beauty is indescribable. Its power is breathtaking. Its potential is unlimited. It comforts the grieving and heals the broken in the context of community. It builds bridges to seekers and offers truth to the confused. It provides resources for those in need and opens its arms to the forgotten, the downtrodden, the disillusioned. It breaks the chains of addictions, frees the oppressed, and offers belonging to the marginalized of this world. Whatever the capacity for human suffering, the church has a greater capacity for healing and wholeness. Still to this day, the potential of the local church is almost more than I can grasp. No other organization on earth is like the church. Nothing even comes close.[6]

This work of mission alignment falls on the leaders of the church. The elders and staff must seek the Lord for a sense of mission for each local church in its context. The purpose of the church remains to worship God. The mission of the church is best expressed by the Great Commission bestowed by Christ himself: "Go therefore and make disciples of all nations, baptizing them in the name of the Father and of the Son and of the Holy Spirit, teaching them to observe all that I have commanded you" (Matthew 28:19-20).

Nevertheless, it is incumbent on every gathered church to apply the purpose and mission of the church to its own setting—to provide the people with vision and strategy, and maybe even a few plans and goals! The best place to begin is to ask, How is the world suffering in our midst, and how can we share in that pain? The role of the church in the world is to bear witness to the Lord, the burden-bearer—the Lamb of God who takes away the sins of the world. Purpose, mission, vision are found where the world hurts and God grieves. Find the vision and make it plain. Happiness withers quickly under the hot sun of suffering when the sense of mission is lost.

Happiness is giving our life to Jesus Christ and being used for his purposes in joyful obedience. Once our life is established in Jesus, once our soul belongs to him, he will begin to give us away to those around us in amazing ways. Not only do we get to experience the happiness of being blessed but we get to experience the wonder of what life can be when we become a blessing to others. Once we give our life away into the hands of the One who has overcome the world, he begins overcoming the world through us. If we think we've felt happy, wait until our life is used as an eternal blessing to someone else. Wait until some gift or talent is used by Jesus to do something eternal. Now that's happiness that can never be taken away!

What is true of the individual Christian must be applied to our life together as a church. The happy church gives itself away to the purposes of Christ. The happy church is sacrificially engaged in the mission of God and marked by joyful obedience.

Songs at a Funeral

Ellen Charry's book *God and the Art of Happiness* provides firm under-pinnings for much of what I've talked about in the previous chapters.

You might wonder why she wanted to engage in such intense study on whether our happiness matters to God. If you pick up that book, you'll see this is serious academic work running from the very beginnings of the church to present day. It is deep study of great theologians from history, with pointed exegetical work in the Hebrew and Greek texts of Scripture. This is no pamphlet on keeping a positive attitude. It's serious work in historical theology.

What made Ellen, my seminary professor, want to study hap-piness to that depth? She did it because her husband—the love of her life and best friend—was diagnosed with lung cancer at the age of fifty-six, though he never smoked. He died that same year, in 2003.

"I was searching for grounds where I could support my life again," she said in an interview. "Happiness took on a whole different meaning to me. It became personal."[7]

We need happiness. We search hard for true foundations of hap-piness when we are buffeted by tragedy and overcome with pain. Remember, Jesus said happy are the sad. "Happy are you who weep now" (Luke 6:21 GNT).

The people heard it and couldn't understand.

The disciples too wished Jesus would make more sense.

But Jesus knew what he was saying.

There is a happiness that grows deeper, stronger, because it is tested by suffering. Its taproot runs so deep that drought causes its roots to grow stronger. Its keel is so far down in the water that the waves demonstrate the strength of the ship as they splash against the side and over the bow.

Charles Spurgeon once said,

There is no cry so good as that which comes from the bottom of the mountains; no prayer half so hearty as that which comes up from the depths of the soul, through deep trials and afflictions. Hence they bring us to God, and we are happier; for that is the way to be happy—to live near to God.[8]

There is a theory that Jesus is such a superstar because he was a great motivational speaker who roused crowds into excitement about a new movement of love and good deeds. Of course, for that to be true, Jesus would have been a motivational speaker of infinite orders of magnitude better than any the world has ever known.

However, it's not highly motivating to be told that you are going to suffer.

Jesus knew well the effect his revelation would have on the world. He knew well the rejection that would descend on him and then on his followers. Jesus knew almost all of his disciples would be given over to death for following him. However, "In the world you will have tribulation. But take heart; I have overcome the world" (John 16:33)!

Happiness is giving our life to Jesus Christ. He has overcome. In him we become world conquerors. We become the happy people of God who sing even at the grave. We become the people of God who are able to laugh at the destruction the world sends, tell jokes around the hospital bed, smile at the greatest disappointments and put joyful confidence in God through the bitter seasons.

To celebrate happiness is not to discount sadness. To take up the mission of joy is not to dismiss the reality of suffering. We need to talk about the happiness that mourns. We need to talk about the smiles and the laughter at the bedside of the dying. We need to know the happiness we are seeking and finding in Christ doesn't burn off like a mist when hardships come. There is a kind of happiness that mourns, but at the very same time it has the power to overcome mourning.

In our funerals we say prayers, some of them stretching back into the beginning of the church, so early they can't be attributed to any one person. There's a line in these prayers that perhaps you've heard: "All of us go down to the dust; yet even at the grave we make our song: Alleluia! Alleluia! Alleluia!"

There is a kind of happiness that mourns, but at the very same time it has the power to overcome mourning.

Who sings "Alleluia" graveside? Who sings "Praise God" standing by the remains of their loved one? I'll never forget one of my first funerals when I was a young associate pastor. My senior pastor, Jonathan Miller, was leading a memorial service at which I offered a reading and a prayer. The sanctuary was full and we were singing *Amazing Grace*. Some were singing loud, but others were just standing stock still or staring out the window. Jonathan leaned over to me and whispered, "See that? Not everyone can sing at a funeral. If you know Christ, you have a song to sing."

Answering the Call

It seems absurd for me to write about the suffering church from my position ensconced in the comforts of the American suburbs. Even as I write, the litany of suffering continues. Iraq has been evacuated of Christians, and Syria is soon to follow. Christians are being driven from their homes, beheaded unceremoniously and literally crucified in the public square. In Garissa, Kenya, Islamic terrorists attacked a Christian fellowship of college students and slaughtered 156 innocent young men and women. Closer to home, Emanuel AME Church in Charleston, South Carolina, has just suffered the racially motivated murder of its pastor and eight others in a Wednesday night Bible study. By the time this book goes to print, these incidents will have been largely forgotten and replaced by further horrors in the ongoing litany of suffering. The suffering of the Christian church is not a light affair.

How can we write of happiness?

The church has always suffered and always will—until the re-newal of all things in the coming kingdom. But as the church bears pain, it also bears witness to the presence of the power of God in its moments of distress.

One of the great privileges of being a pastor is that families let me in on their most intimate and painful moments. I can't tell you how many bedsides I have stood by praying with families as loved ones take their final breaths. I've been privileged to be there in the suffering.

Why is it a privilege? Because something happens in those places that no one—not even the families—talks about: we laugh. Not always, but when Jesus is there and his Spirit is present, hap-piness is found in the midst of tears.

There are jokes that only chemotherapy patients can make with one another in the treatment room. There are smiles and giggles only the sufferers can share. The presence of the Lord is there in the midst of struggle and sadness, and it is so mysterious the world cannot see or understand it. The laughs, the jokes, the smirks—the prayers, hugs and smiles through wet cheeks—they are more precious than gold.

A few years ago a number of devastating tornadoes ripped through Missouri killing 158 people and causing $2.8 billion in damage. Joplin was virtually wiped off the map. Helicopter flyovers revealed a swath of destruction; it looked like a giant lawnmower was pushed through the middle of town, over neighborhoods, churches and schools without discrimination.

I watched a man interviewed on TV the next day. The inter-viewer was trying to make hay out of the depth of human misery, and the victim simply would not play the role. As this man was being interviewed, he started to laugh. "The whole thing's gone, can you believe it?" he said, smiling at the reporter.

The newsperson seemed perturbed by this and asked him, "Sir, how can you take this so lightly?"

"Well, we cry a lot too," he said, "but you might as well laugh! It's in the Lord's hands."

You might as well take joy. You might as well march confidently through the lions' den. You might as well smile boldly in the face of affliction. You might as well shake the gates of hell with a defiant song of God's glory. You might as well. It's in the Lord's hands. God even seems to provide the power to do it.

In my first year at my current church, north Georgia was hit by devastating tornadoes. We gathered a team of men to respond. Being the church means responding to the needs of the world—particularly the pain. None of us wanted our days to be interrupted. None of us wanted our schedules pushed and our other responsibilities to pile up. But we went. We responded to the mission to bring joy to those in need. In this case it was in the form of water, groceries and chainsaws.

We were sad to see the destruction and to share the feeling of insecurity. But the Lord filled us with joy and laughter as we worked. In the end we all felt so happy that we had done it. We suffered the mission of joy, and God filled us with gladness.

Half of it was the stories we had to tell.

Answer the call to the mission, the mission to bring joy to the pain, and see if God doesn't meet you there with happiness.

I once set up our youth group for a mission trip to Camden when I served a church in southern New Jersey. "You'll get letters on this one," I was told. "You can take kids to the border of Mexico, you can take them to the slums of Nairobi, but you try to take them to Camden and you will see fire shoot out of the eyes of these parents."

It didn't turn out that bad, but my mission director was right. Parents in that area of New Jersey did not want their kids in Camden, even though it was only thirty minutes away. I got a letter. "Don't you know that every kid who dies of a drug overdose in our county gets those drugs from Camden?" I wanted to say, "Don't you know every drug dealer in Camden gets his money from your rich suburban kids?" But I didn't. I just took the kids to Camden.

Our church was growing in mission. We had been to Mexico and Kenya and the Dominican Republic, but the real challenge was joining forces with UrbanPromise in Camden (urbanpromiseusa.org). I was not the vanguard on this. Actually, the mission director and the senior pastor had led the way with the church's involvement in local mission. But to bring the kids to Camden, that was a new challenge!

The suffering is never far. The world is broken, right up to the door of the church, right through that door and all the way in. It's not hard to find the suffering. It's hard to find the courage to take up the mission of joy.

That church's relationship with UrbanPromise is now one of the most important aspects of its character. I think they derive

> **It's not hard to find the suffering. It's hard to find the courage to take up the mission of joy.**

more joy from that relationship than any other.

Light Shines in the Darkness

John Ortberg relays the story of his father-in-law's conversion. Al was a classic hunter-gatherer tough guy, and for years John had a hard time relating to him. But then Al got pancreatic cancer. Somehow, in the midst of the suffering and tears, there was room for Christ to move in.

One day John's mother asked Al if he should die before she does, what would he want the grandkids to know about God from their grandparents. (These are the ingenious questions of persistent evangelists.) It led to an opportunity to open the Bible with him and explain the love of God. With a little bit more conversation, searching the Scriptures and some prayer, "the light dawned, the ice melted, and Al prayed and gave his life to God."[9] It opened Al's heart for serious changes. He had always been slow to say "I love

you" to his daughter. One day John heard Nancy, his wife, finishing
a conversation with her dad when she said something he had never
heard: "I love you too, Dad." Reflecting on the end of Al's life much
later, John writes, "The darkest year of his life became, somehow,
the year of light."[10]

Later, when John entered a period of suffering and disappointment in his own life, he went to his spiritual mentor and
friend Dallas Willard and poured out his soul as he had done so
many times before. Dallas, in his wisdom, said to him, "This will
be a test of your joyful confidence in God."[11] John realized it was
time to trust God in the suffering. Not just with an intellectual
confidence but with a "joyful confidence." It was time to believe his
well-being, the eternal status of his soul, his identity and all his
hopes and dreams belong to God the Father of our Lord Jesus
Christ—and this God can be trusted.

When we have that kind of trust in God, the moments or
seasons or even years of suffering become occasions for growing
deeper roots of joy, happiness, peace, contentment and confidence
in the steadfast love of Jesus. When we give our life to the one who
can redeem it, we will know the great reversal of the cross. This is
what happens when our life passes through the paradox of the
crucified Savior. The suffering becomes blessing. The sadness becomes an occasion for an uplifted spirit. Our sorrow turns into joy.

There is an old saying: "The same sun that melts the ice hardens
the clay." Suffering will come. The question is, what effect will it
have on your soul? Will it soften your heart or harden your spirit?
Will it serve to drive you closer to Jesus or push you farther away?

How can the happy church be happy in the midst of tears? It
can do just that because it holds a deep secret, a "magic deeper
still," to borrow from C. S. Lewis's Aslan.[12] We are happy in tears
because we know the suffering is not without purpose, and neither
will it prevail, but the eternal kingdom is presently emerging,

guaranteed by a victory already won. The smile under the stream of tears bears witness to this truth.

The church can take courage. It can boldly move toward suffering. Our prayers can move us into the pain of the world around us with confidence. Our God is bigger than the pain. "The light shines in the darkness, and the darkness has not overcome it" (John 1:5).

The Future Feast We Taste

"O taste and see that the Lord is good; blessed is the man who trusts in him" (Psalm 34:8), for God never disappoints the expectations of those who seek his favor. Our own unbelief is the only impediment which prevents him from satisfying us largely and bountifully with abundance of all good things.

JOHN CALVIN

• • •

There will be pie!"

Last year my church decided to forgo ordinary Sunday morning worship on Father's Day for a single service of worship in the local park: "Church in the Park!" Making the announcement about it, I was joking around a little when off-the-cuff I said, "And I hope there will be a few pies. The world needs more pie."

Turns out there are a lot of bakers in my church. And they have been unable to share pie with the church since we moved from potluck suppers to catered meals. There was a backlog on church pies. When I looked at the food setup, an entire spread—two picnic tables long—was filled with pies!

God not only wants the church to know he is good, God wants the church to sense it, to feel and experience that he is good—to taste and see.

The Holy Spirit in the community of faith gives us a foretaste of the feast of the kingdom. The happy church knows this feeling. It knows the taste of the kingdom. And it knows how to celebrate what it tastes.

Jonathan Edwards said there's a big difference between hearing or even knowing that God is good and actually tasting that God is good.

> Thus there is a difference between having an opinion, that God is holy and gracious, and having a sense of the loveliness and beauty of that holiness and grace. There is a difference between having a rational judgment that honey is sweet, and having a sense of its sweetness.[1]

The senses must be engaged.

Origen of Alexandria, an early church father, believed the Holy Spirit grants Christians a spiritual set of senses, and the Scriptures are full of examples. Spiritual sight enables us to see things others don't. Spiritual hearing allows us to hear things (like the voice of God from heaven) without sound waves produced by a material body. Perhaps there is even "a taste which feeds on living bread that has come down from heaven and gives life to the world."[2] Origen argued for a set of five spiritual senses every bit as real as the five physical senses allowing us to experience the things of God. I'm not sure we need to subscribe entirely to this, but no doubt part of the purpose of church is to engage the senses with the qualities of the kingdom.

How does God engage our senses? He knows we need to do more than think, to experience as much as we consider—we need to taste and see. This comes from the Holy Spirit.

The Holy Spirit is mysterious. Jesus even said so—it's like the wind: we see it blowing but we never really know where it comes from or where it's going. The Nicene Creed originally declared,

And [we believe] in the Holy Spirit, the Lord and life-giver, who proceeds from the Father, who with the Father and the Son is together worshipped and together glorified, who spoke through the prophets; in one holy catholic and apostolic church; we confess one baptism to the remission of sins; we look forward to the resurrection of the dead and the life of the world to come.[3]

Sometimes we understand this to mean we believe in the Holy Spirit, and then we also believe in these other things on the list. But a better way to understand it is that we believe in the Holy Spirit, the cause and source of the rest of these things on the list. We don't put our trust in the church the same way we put our trust in the Father, Son and Holy Spirit. This last part of the creed is an outline of all the activities of the Holy Spirit among us in the community of faith.

The Spirit makes the church the church. The Spirit is God, who spoke through the prophets—that's another way of saying the Holy Spirit inspires the Scriptures. Because of the Holy Spirit we have the Bible. The Holy Spirit gathers the church, the church *catholic* (which means everywhere and every time—universal) and *apostolic* (which means rightfully teaching and preaching the gospel Jesus gave the apostles to preach). The Spirit does this. The Spirit is what makes baptism *baptism* and makes Holy Communion, well, *holy*! As one church father said, to paraphrase, "Nobody makes holy like the Holy Spirit makes holy."[4] Then we have "the resurrection of the dead, and the life of the world to come." The Holy Spirit makes resurrection happen and seals the guarantee of the coming kingdom on our hearts (Ephesians 1:13-14).

The Spirit does all these things. The truth is, without the Holy Spirit, there is no church. Nothing we see in the happy church could occur—not for one day, not for one minute—apart from the power of the Holy Spirit.

The happy church is full of the Spirit of God. We need to learn to talk more about his power, to pray for it and to fill our tanks with it. The Spirit is the Lord, the Giver of life. And his presence is a party.

> **Nothing we see in the happy church could occur—not for one day, not for one minute—apart from the power of the Holy Spirit.**

The Potluck, Where Everyone Brings a Taste

When I think of a church party, I immediately think of potluck suppers.

I have good memories of them from when I was a kid in Colorado Springs. I was always gunning for the Jell-O molds, particularly those with miniature marshmallows. Long tables were set up against the wall in the church basement. We entered from the back door. There was no need to use the formal front doors; it was just us.

Family by family, with steaming pots and baskets and pans with tinfoil, we marched in and took our positions at the tables. Each crock told a story about the household it came from. "Oh yeah, I forgot they lived in Germany." "I suppose she found that on her mission trip to Africa." There were three different pans of fried chicken, five types of dinner rolls, multiple green-bean casseroles and six different pies. One woman watched her avocados with deep concern, sorry they had turned brown. Her friends worked to console her while another group bickered about how long the potato salad should stay out.

The tables reflected the people. The Millers were from Michigan, the Moraleses had moved from Alamosa, the Georgettis from New Jersey, the McClures from Arkansas; the Paynes had recently moved from Phoenix, and the Yiums had just been relocated from

Portland. My family was from Tennessee, although you couldn't tell any longer by our softened accent. Hardly anyone was raised in Colorado. Together we ate around tables like a family.

Adults tried to engage in conversation while we kids tried our luck at grabbing another roll or a third brownie. Soon, the boys disappeared outside to the playground hidden in the woods. Eventually, we were called back to head home. Empty bowls and crocks made their way back into the car. Everything ran much later than expected. We were tired but satisfied.

It was a very simple exercise. Normal in many respects. But looking back on it I know we had tasted a little bit of the feast of Revelation, the marriage supper of the Lamb, where there will be "a great multitude that no one could number, from every nation, from all tribes and peoples and languages, standing before the throne and before the Lamb" (Revelation 7:9). As Jesus promised, "people will come from east and west, and from north and south, and recline at table in the kingdom of God" (Luke 13:29).

The Holy Spirit, the Lord, the Giver of life—organizer of a potluck?

"Did you taste that yet? That's good! Try that!"

It's the power of the potluck. The happy church multiplies by simple joy. At its fathomless center, the hidden core of the happy church is a reservoir of deep joy and gladness bubbling up in the most ordinary events. A humble church meal is a party like no other, foreshadowing the coming feast of the Bridegroom in the eternity of the heavens.

My friend John is now the pastor of a church of nations. Like many suburban churches, it went through a season of anxiety when their neighborhood demographics changed. They were used to being homogenous, but the neighborhood was becoming a rich plurality of peoples. John led the way, pastoring that church through a complete transformation into multiethnic ministry. Every time a family from a new nationality or heritage joins the church, they raise a flag in the lobby. There are twenty-three flags so far.

John says, "Tim, our potlucks are awesome. You can't believe the variety of tastes. You've never seen so many different types of food. It's like a taste-of-nations festival every time we gather!"

When Pentecost came, the Spirit blew on that small gathering with explosive force (Acts 2). The word for power in Greek is *dynamis*, where we get the word *dynamite*. Boom! They were filled with the Spirit's power and their tongues were loosed. They could tell anybody, from any land, about Jesus. It was supernaturally easy to talk about Jesus, and it was supernaturally easy for the gospel to be understood and received. They were empowered.

You know what else? They were together: "When the day of Pentecost arrived, they were all together in one place" (Acts 2:1). They had come from everywhere, but there they were together.

The church was all together; the church was empowered. Same thing. When the church comes together under the power of the Holy Spirit, there is energy, excitement and joy. A meal is a symbol, a reenactment of the spiritual reality when a church—together—decides to find what the Spirit is doing and be a part of it.

What kind of potluck do you find in a church like that? It feels good to be together. It feels empowering to be all together, each bringing something to the table for others to enjoy. In a sense, every meal becomes a sacramental meal.

The King's Decree

From time to time in Scripture, God graciously gives us a glimpse of the future, a foreshadowing of how it all turns out. These glimpses have enormous power. They are like lightning flashes across a darkened field—one burst and for a split second we see it all, then back into darkness. This is the promise. The direction everything is headed.

Isaiah 24 is a scene in God's throne room. It reveals the Lord on the glory seat of his kingdom:

The LORD of hosts reigns
  on Mount Zion and in Jerusalem,
  and his glory will be before his elders. (Isaiah 24:23)

God takes his place on the high mount of his own sovereignty and calls the elders around him: "Come in. Gather around. I have something to say."

This is the throne room, the court of the King, where he makes his great decrees, where his declarations and judgments come down. An important and authoritative announcement is coming. It's a proclamation from God on high.

When the US president has something to say, we kind of know what's coming according to where he makes the announcement. The TV splashes "Special Report: President Addresses the Nation." Then the picture fades in and we see the setting. If he's in the Rose Garden, maybe someone special is being recognized or a monumental piece of legislation is being ceremoniously signed into law. If he's in the pressroom, he's probably cleaning up a mess. ("Whatever I said, I meant the opposite!") But if the president is sitting behind his desk in the Oval Office . . . "Oh no. This is serious. We're going to war!"

In Isaiah's vision the elders are gathered in the glory of the Lord, who is seated on Mount Zion. Imagine the uneasy apprehension: "What's he going to say? What's happening? What is this proclamation? Are we going to war? Are we in financial collapse? What is it?"

The King opens his mouth and makes his declaration: "On this mountain the LORD of hosts will make for all peoples a feast!" (Isaiah 25:6). There will be a *feast*!

The mighty King, with all his authority and glory on display in the most demonstrative and commanding way, makes the solemn declaration: "On my word there will be joy!"

"A feast of rich food, a feast of well-aged wine, of rich food full of marrow, of aged wine well refined!" (Isaiah 25:6). This is what the Lord proclaims; the Lord God Almighty declares the feast! That's the mighty promise. That's the King's decree.

> **The mighty King, with all his authority and glory on display in the most demonstrative and commanding way, makes the solemn declaration: "On my word there will be joy!"**

How do we miss this?

Is Christianity a dour and bitter drink: all suffering and self-abasement and embarrassment, until one day we are pinned down behind the glass in some holy museum called "heaven"?

No!

God promises a *party*. Between now and then there will be struggles, but the King has declared a celebration. The feast is guaranteed on the word of the Lord God Almighty, the Lord of hosts. There are bitter cups to drink—none so bitter as the cup our Lord drank in Gethsemane. But the bitter cup he drank there, he drank to guarantee the rich wine we will drink in his kingdom. You see? The Lord has declared the feast.

> And he will swallow up on this mountain
>   the covering that is cast over all peoples,
>   the veil that is spread over all nations.
> He will swallow up death forever;
> and the Lord GOD will wipe away tears from all faces,
>   and the reproach of his people he will take away from all
>   the earth,
> for the LORD has spoken. (Isaiah 25:7-8)

This is the declaration of the King from on high. For the Lord has spoken.

What then? On that day we will stand and say,

Behold, this is our God; we have waited for him, that he might save us.
>   This is the LORD; we have waited for him;
>   let us be glad and rejoice in his salvation. (Isaiah 25:9)

Yes, this is the Lord. This is the character of God. This is who God is: the God who declares the *feast*. We waited for him. There's something in our soul that knew it all along: God is loving, God is good, God is our refuge. He is a safe place and our good Father in heaven. Yes. This is the Lord, and our soul has been waiting for him.

Repeat it once more: "This is our God" (Isaiah 25:9). Behold, *this* is our God. Get it? *I've suffered a thousand false notions of who God is, but now I see him.* The lies have been repeated, so let's repeat the truth once more. This is God. This is our God! Can you see him? The Lord of the feast.

I love each year when all the Christmas movies roll out. *Elf. Christmas Vacation. The Christmas Story.* I watch them all. But my favorite character is from Charles Dickens's *A Christmas Carol*— good old Mr. Fezziwig.

> Old Fezziwig laid down his pen, and looked up at the clock, which pointed to the hour of seven. He rubbed his hands, laughed all over himself, from his shoes to his organ of benevolence, and called out, in a comfortable, oily, rich, fat, jovial voice: "Yo ho, my boys! No more work tonight. Christmas Eve, Dick. Christmas, Ebenezer!"[5]

Old Fezziwig declared the feast. In came the musicians, up came the dances, out came the maidens, the cold roast, the boiled port, the mince pies, the cake and plenty of beer.

"A small thing," says the angel to Ebenezer Scrooge. The whole party probably cost a few pounds sterling.

"No small thing!" argues Ebenezer. "He has the power to render us happy or unhappy. . . . The happiness he gives, is quite as great as if it cost a fortune."[6]

The feast Fezziwig declares makes room in Ebenezer's cold and sin-gripped heart. It makes room for the conversion he is about to experience. It doesn't cost much to provide invaluable happiness.

That's our God. God declares the feast, and the promise of joy is enough to make our hearts believe.

> Behold, this is our God; we have waited for him, that he might save us.
> This is the LORD; we have waited for him;
> let us be glad and rejoice in his salvation. (Isaiah 25:9)

The Feast Will Not Be Stopped

In 1986 the Beastie Boys, an American hip-hop band, became so rich overnight that they never had to work again! What song did it? "(You Gotta) Fight for Your Right (to Party!)." There's a bit of truth to that.

The party never comes without resistance. Somebody has to stand up and declare the feast and fight for the party—fight for the joy of the community against all resistance.

The parable of the prodigal son (Luke 15) is one of the most famous in the Scriptures. A father has two sons. The younger son demands his inheritance while the father is still alive. Remarkably, the father grants his son his wish. The son takes his inheritance and squanders it on loose living. This rebellious son then finds himself bottoming out, feeding pigs slop, which he would like eat himself since he's so hungry. Jesus says at that moment the young man "comes to himself" and realizes he should go home. Before he reaches the door, the father runs into the street to meet him and calls the servants to slaughter the fattened calf. There will be joy. There will be a feast! The lost son is home.

The story, like many parables of Jesus, reveals the character of God through a metaphor: the picture of this loving, forgiving, sacrificing father. And the father in our parable knew what it meant to fight for the celebration. His goal would not be frustrated. Nothing could stand in the way of the father's feast. Every sacrifice he makes is headed in one direction: the party, the feast, the completion of the drama when everyone comes home, restored, celebrated—happy.

The father first endures horrendous insult when the younger son demands his inheritance before the father has passed away. But he endures it; he sacrifices. Jesus says he divided the property. It's worth noting that in the Greek language "property" is the word *bios*, which means "life." In Greek that's how someone would talk about the sum total of his estate, his farm and his livelihood.[7] Jesus' listeners wouldn't miss that the father split up his own life (*bios*) to give what his reckless son demands. He sacrifices.

Next, when the son has done his thing and is on his way home, the father catches a glimpse of him while he is still far off. In a moment, the father is up from his seat and running toward his son, whom he loves. In ancient Middle Eastern culture it was shameful for the patriarch to run like this.[8] He would have to lift up his cloak, baring his ankles and knees, and run like a schoolboy. Dishonorable. But his love drives him. He sacrifices.

Then the embrace. He should have stood stern and unbending, waiting for the supplication of his errant son. On the way home, the son has been rehearsing what he will say: "I will arise and go to my father, and I will say to him, 'Father, I have sinned against heaven and before you. I am no longer worthy to be called your son. Treat me as one of your hired servants'" (Luke 15:18-19). The son's rehearsed speech is right. It's the truth. He has sinned. He has broken covenant. He has shamed and embarrassed his father. He has lost his right to be called a son. All that is true. But the father won't have any of it because loving forgiveness trumps the truth of the son's confession.

The son has a debt to pay. The debt cannot be dismissed as insignificant or of no account, but the father retains the right to contend with that debt according to his own will.

Pastor Tim Keller writes,

> Over the years people have drawn the superficial conclusion that the restoration of the younger brother came at no cost, that it involved no atonement. They point out that the younger son wanted to make restitution but the father wouldn't let him— his acceptance back into the family was simply free. This, they say, shows that forgiveness and love should always be free and unconditional. That is an oversimplification. . . . [If someone wrongs you,] the forgiveness is free and unconditional to the perpetrator, but it is costly to you. Mercy and forgiveness must be free and unmerited to the wrongdoer. If the wrongdoer has to do something to merit it, then it isn't mercy, but forgiveness *always* comes at a cost to the one granting the forgiveness.[9]

The prodigal son didn't come home free. The cost was great—but it wasn't paid by him. The cost was enormous, more than he could ever pay. It was paid by the sacrifice of another.

Something of the mystery of God's grace is revealed in this story. God's character is proven to be extravagant, overwhelming love. Love at any cost. And this love is not just for the lost younger brother. The father's grace is yet to be fully tried; the older brother won't join the party. The father has to walk out of the party, where he sits as host and master, and go into the dark night to beg his older son to join them.

God's character is proven to be extravagant, overwhelming love. Love at any cost.

The father loves both of these boys. Both of these children are loved with extravagance and sacrifice. And why does the father endure so much pain and sacrifice? What is it all for? The end of the story is the *feast*. The father is intent on reconciliation with his sons and will not stop sacrificing and struggling until that peace is found. The father is the hero, and the hero fights until the victory is won and all resolves to joyful celebration.

At every turn the father pictures the coming feast. He is intent on the celebration of joy. He is fixated on the future, when his children are restored to his love. That's what motivates him to endure another sacrifice and another and another—this coming joy and happiness and restoration and fulfillment and redemption *will not be taken from the father!* No way.

This is our God.

"On my word there will be joy."

The Feast Requires Sacrifice

The feast is present in many of Jesus' parables, foreshadowed in the institution of Communion in Paul's letters and again in the apocalyptic visions of the end of time in Revelation. We will join in *the* feast with God, and this feast is guaranteed.

In the parable of the prodigal son the father sends for the fattened calf to be sacrificed. This is no little command. As a culture we are so separated from our meat production that we can't relate to this. When the lord of the house calls for the calf to be slaughtered, it means someone has to harvest the meat. There is a painful blow, a struggle and work enough to tire a man. There are knives, skin, blood and fur.

People of Jesus' day didn't eat meat at every meal but only a few times a year. When a calf was slaughtered, the doors were opened for all to join the celebration and eat meat.

On my first trip to Kenya we were honored to be part of a house blessing. Our friends Peter and Esther had built a new house in their town and planned a party to dedicate it to the service of the Lord. They roasted three goats for the celebration. I was astounded at how many people showed up for the party—they kept coming out of the woodwork.

"Who's been invited to this thing?" I asked Peter. He looked at me quizzically, not really understanding the question.

"Everyone is invited. Anyone who can smell the goat roasting!"

That's the kind of feast the father in the parable is holding. All are invited because the calf is already killed. The blood of the animal has already hit the floor. It will not be wasted. The festival is guaranteed by the spilling of blood.

Do you see? It's the same with Jesus. Tim Keller writes, "So too at the end of the book of Revelation, at the end of history, there is a feast, the 'marriage supper of the Lamb' (Revelation 19). The Lamb is Jesus, who was sacrificed for the sins of the world so that we could be pardoned and brought home."[10] The blood has already been spilled. The price for our forgiveness has been paid, and by that blood a covenant has been made.

"There will be joy in my house," says the Lord.

This future, guaranteed feast tells us something about our relationship with Christ right now. If a feast of celebration is coming at the end, what about our relationship with Christ right now? Is it a dry, pallid, tasteless relationship? Then something is missing. Christ brings music, dancing, joy, good food, beauty, truth, happiness—even in the midst of despair the feast can be present in Christ.

Sometimes it's hard to believe we are invited to the feast. It's hard to believe the feast is coming and the Lord intends to see us dance. It's hard to believe when life hands us a raw deal. When we feel injustice. When a child is born with a disability. When cancer emerges. When a parent starts to fall into the fog of Alzheimer's.

It's hard to believe when the floods rise and take our home, when the winds whip and flatten our town and all we know. It's hard to believe in the feast of the Father. But we've got to fight a little bit. Fight for our right. The party is coming.

Happy church, God intends to see you dance. The blood has been spilled, the covenant has been ratified, the party will happen, and the Father's feast will not be frustrated.

It is coming! Every party we hold is a rehearsal. The true party is on the way.

When the Church
Is Heaven's Sunlight

You can lead us to heaven if you have got
heaven's sunlight on your face.

CHARLES SPURGEON

• • •

Cyprian was born to a wealthy family in a nice part of the Roman Empire—Carthage, on the northern coast of Africa. Even though he tasted the best the world had to offer in the second century, the world seemed to him a harsh place. Shortly before his death, he wrote to his neighbor Donatus to explain why he became a Christian.

Cyprian and Donatus were both sons of fortune, living comfortable lives full of garden parties, wine and philosophy while the world "out there" was a hard place full of injustice and pain. "The whole world is wet with mutual blood; and murder. . . . Cruelty is perpetrated on a grand scale," Cyprian wrote to Donatus.[1] The cities are full of sadness and solitude, and gladiators perform to satisfy the lust of cruel eyes, there is a general collapse of morals and piety, and the most celebrated person is the one who produces the largest spectacle of human degradation: "Their crimes become their religion." The rich feed on the poor, the powerless are oppressed by their masters, and arguments are won by those who shout the loudest. In short, it is a brutal and amoral world dragging the soul down to the gutter, said Cyprian.

But with God, Cyprian believed, the soul could be elevated beyond all these things and given the Spirit's power to transcend the evils of the present age.

It's stunning to hear the echoes of a former time resonating in our own. A later biographer summarized the letter this way:

> Donatus, this is a cheerful world indeed as I see it from my fair garden, under the shadow of my vines. But if I could ascend some high mountain, and look out over the wide lands, you know very well what I should see: brigands on the highways, pirates on the seas, armies fighting, cities burning, in the amphitheaters men murdered to please applauding crowds, selfishness and cruelty and misery and despair under all roofs. It is a bad world, Donatus, an incredibly bad world. But I have discovered in the midst of it a company of quiet and holy people who have learned a great secret. They have found a joy which is a thousand times better than any of the pleasures of our sinful life. They are despised and persecuted, but they care not: they are masters of their souls. They have overcome the world. These people, Donatus, are the Christians,—and I am one of them.[2]

Cyprian was called to this happy, joyful society with Christ and proved willing to defend it with his life. When the edict came down that all should sacrifice to the emperor as if to a god, he refused. He was arrested and tried. The officer of the court read the final verdict: "Thascius Cyprian is sentenced to die by the sword." Cyprian simply replied, "Thanks be to God."[3]

A World Hungry for Heaven

What's the world really like? It's brutal. People know this. The world is filled with scandal and shame, selfishness and greed, bitterness and human degradation. Cyprian was right. It's a dark and messy world. And do you know what? Not a single soul is satisfied with the way the world is. Not one.

We are hungry for heaven, starving for the justice of God.

In *Mere Christianity*, C. S. Lewis addresses the human hunger for heaven. No matter how sweet life is in this world, no matter how successful the job, how warm the marriage, how perfect the summer vacation, there is nevertheless something missing, "something that cannot be had in this world. . . . Something has evaded us." There are a few ways to deal with this longing. The fool's way is to try more expensive holidays, a new spouse, a better job, expecting different results. The disillusioned way is to become a sensible adult, dismissing the longing as a juvenile quest and abandoning all hope of ultimate happiness. About this way, Lewis writes, "It would be the best line we could take if man did not live for ever. But supposing infinite happiness really is there, waiting for us?" Then this supposedly sophisticated apathy is truly tragic.

The way Lewis commends is the Christian way:

> The Christian says, "Creatures are not born with desires unless satisfaction for those desires exists. A baby feels hunger: well, there is such a thing as food. A duckling wants to swim: well, there is such a thing as water. Men feel sexual desire: well, there is such a thing as sex. If I find in myself a desire which no experience in this world can satisfy, the most probable explanation is that I was made for another world."[4]

We are all dissatisfied with this world. We are fit for heaven. This

> **Not a single soul is satisfied with the way the world is. Not one.**

is the state of all people—unquiet and disturbed by this world, we all want something more. God has planted eternity in our hearts, and we want it. We demand it! Our souls will not be quiet until they come home to Jesus.

In a world like this, people want to be part of something different. They want to be part of something bigger. They long to find a community devoted to a higher ethic, a higher cause, a different world.

They want the church. Their hearts were made by God, for God. God made them in such a way that praising him would bring them joy. Their hearts will be unquiet until they rest in Christ their Savior. What they want is a community to attest to this; a community of happy souls resting contentedly in the hands of Christ.

This being the case, we must ask ourselves why the dissatisfied and unquiet souls of our era have no interest in church. There are many reasons, but chief among them is that we Christians are not acting like those who know the solution. We do not present ourselves as a people who know peace with God and who rest content in the midst of a discontented world. We don't act like the happy church. Our behavior does not match our true identity.

The world needs to find a happy community of people whose God is the Lord! The world needs to see the peace and joy of a people in pursuit of Christ, saved by the mighty hand of God. As missionary Lesslie Newbigin has written, "the only effective hermeneutic of the gospel is the life of the congregation which believes it."[5] The only way to translate the gospel to the darkened world around us is to be the people of good news.

The only way to translate the gospel to the darkened world around us is to be the people of good news.

If you don't want to be happy for yourself, if you still find it ignoble to pursue happiness on your own account, then be happy *for* the world. The world needs to see the happiness of the community of faith. Be happy *for* those who are lost. Be happy on behalf of the miserable. They need to know there is a source of joy deeper than the wells of the world and its pleasures. Be happy *for* them so they can be found. They need it. They are looking for the light of heaven.

The joy we share as the people of God and the exuberance we are able to produce are like heaven's sunlight on our face. And the world cannot do without it.

Eyes Are Watching

The lighthouse keeper has one job: keep the flame lit and the light shining.

If your church is starting to shine a little brighter in happiness, if this pursuit of joy has helped you feel happier about the light your church is sending into the world, then you had better be prepared to guard the light of heaven.

Charles Spurgeon, London's most popular preacher of the nineteenth century, knew people were watching him and measuring his preaching, but he also knew people were watching his congregation. Would the church demonstrate the truth of the surpassing joy of knowing Jesus?

Spurgeon addressed the older generation in his church encouraging them not to grow grumpy with old age: "Do not let the young people catch you indulging in melancholy, sitting in your chimney corner, grumbling and growling, but go about cheerful and happy, and they will think how blessed it is to be a Christian." He warned them that their surliness or irritability could make younger people think that God abandons us in old age.

> You can lead us to heaven if you have got heaven's sunlight on your face; but you will not lead us at all if you are cross and ill-tempered, for then we shall not care about your company.

Make yourselves merry with the people of God, and try to live happily before men; for so will you prove to us—to a demonstration, that even to old age God is with you, and that when your strength faileth, he is still your preservation.[6]

Eyes are ever on you! Keep up the battle. Try to be cheerful. Fight for the happy church. Others are watching to see if it's true, to see what difference the Spirit of Jesus makes in a person. They want to see if the gospel changes men and women and keeps their disposition elevated to things spiritual. Your children are watching; your grandchildren are watching. You can lead them to heaven "if you have got heaven's sunlight on your face."

It takes commitment. It takes a serious commitment to maintain a community of joy. It means taking joy into account, measuring happiness as an indicator of spiritual formation.

Staying Happy Through Change

Leaders can't make every decision based on the immediate happiness of those they lead. But if their decisions are in obedience to Christ, there will be an overriding and continuing joy, and it will be possible to show the church the upward slope that is coming after the valley of change. It is possible to cultivate and defend a culture of joy—even in the midst of difficult challenges.

Your church is going to change. Either it innovates to meet the challenge of bringing the gospel to the next generation or it dies. Either way, it will change. Emptying out and dying is change. Ironically, it's change that comes from leaders resisting the challenges of change. Change is inevitable.

I was recently at a conference for cutting-edge pastors. I sat down for lunch at a table of ministers I had never met. The whole course of the conversation surrounded one topic: pews. Not where to get some. How to get rid of them!

"Did you do it yet?" one pastor ask another. "Did you get rid of the pews?"

"Not yet, but we started the discussion last month."

"I was lucky," said another. "The pastor before me got rid of them and took all the heat."

"Yep, we're removing ours this summer."

I was a little bit blown away. It turns out I'm not all that cutting edge. I have no interest in pew wars.

But let's take that as an example. A young pastor rolls in, and within a year or two the discussion emerges: "They're taking away the pews. This new pastor says no growing church in North America has pews."

"That's ridiculous! He's an idiot. When we put those pews in, attendance doubled."

"Right, he doesn't know what he's talking about. When did we get those pews again?"

"1953, I think. Hard to remember exactly."

That's the moment you get to decide. What do you want to fight for? Change is coming—which means the fight is coming. The wheels move forward, and consequently the friction begins. What do you want to fight for when your church faces change?

Some choose to fight for the past. They resolve to stave off these new ideas, interrupt this new pastor and the innovations he brings, and keep things the way they were.

Think about this. Do you want your reputation, your epithet, to be "We kept things the way they were"? If you win the day, the new pastor will get frustrated and leave. Then the church can hire a pastor in the closing years of ministry, one who agrees that things today should be just as they were thirty years ago. The pews get emptier—but at least we have the pews.

Some choose to fight for the future. Down with the old guard! Innovation is the only way. Newer is always better, and the ways of yesterday must be discarded simply on the basis of age.

Is this the reputation you want? Is that the example you want to set for your children? Push the aged out; newer is always better. My mind is closed to the wisdom of the past. Soon you'll be on the other side of that push: sooner than you think.

Here's what I want us to fight for: fight for *joy*. Fight for gladness. Resolve that you will not jump into the polarizing battle. Resolve that you will wear a cloak of happiness, a mantle of laughter. Fight to remind the church that at the center of its fellowship is joy in communion with Christ. Immerse yourselves in the song of the happy people of God. Demand that the feast be called. Lift the flag of hope. Did the soldier before you fall? Don't let the flag of hope lay lifeless. Lift it up, though you may get struck as you raise it out of the mud and over the rampart. Be a warrior of joy. A captain of gladness. This is serious business, not clowning around. Fight for the happy church.

If you are a church member, you can choose to be an advocate for happiness. If you are an elder or deacon, you have a responsibility to defend it.

I come from a tradition that values church discipline—at least historically. John Knox, a founder of the Presbyterian Church, wrote there are three marks of the true kirk, the true church. (He was Scottish, if you can't hear the brogue yet.) The kirk, he said, is marked by the gospel *r-r-rightly* preached, the sacraments *r-r-rightly* administered and the discipline of the church *r-r-rightly* upheld.

If you are a church member, you can choose to be an advocate for happiness. If you are an elder or deacon, you have a responsibility to defend it.

What does discipline mean? In short, that the fellowship deserves to be protected by its leaders and elders. That while we cast the net wide and fill the halls with grace to make a safe place for all to be themselves, nevertheless the community has table rules.

Throughout the letters of the New Testament, we are told to avoid those who cause divisions and discontent, and instead to strive for unity and oneness of spirit. One disruptive and contrary man, Diotrephes, is actually named for posterity (3 John 9). He is forever remembered for disrespecting the appointed authorities of the church. What a sad and unfortunate legacy. Perhaps the heaviest teaching comes in Titus 3:10, "As for a person who stirs up division, after warning him once and then twice, have nothing to do with him."

Although the church is open to all, and any who have faith in Christ will be made a part of the family of God forever, the fellowship of the local congregation is a privilege, not a right. We are called to be cheerful and loving in the table rules of the community. If we are habitually grumpy, incessantly negative and persistently nasty to those around us in the church, we should not be surprised when a biblically minded elder or pastor confronts us.

Paul and the Holy Spirit seem to be saying that the gladness and joy of the community is too important. The reservoirs of happiness in the community of faith can easily be exhausted on one contentious spirit. Each of us is responsible for our actions, and that includes the projection of our moods. It is our duty to offer gladness to the community of faith as much as we are able. The witness of the church to the world may depend on it.

Not Natural but Possible

Tim Keller claims most people in the world take one of two positions on happiness. The first believes happiness is the natural state of a person, which we are entitled to. In this case, we rail against anything or anyone that hinders our personal happiness. The second position believes happiness is impossible and therefore gives up on its pursuit. When we take this perspective, we descend into apathy marked by sarcasm, cynicism and isolating negativity.

The Christian point of view is different: "The Bible says, and Christians who understand what the Bible says believe, that happiness is neither natural nor unachievable. It's possible. It's possible to be in this world a fundamentally and consistently happy person."[7]

No it isn't a right, and no it isn't inherently achievable, but it is possible! But it must come to us from without. It is not within the range of our own natural capabilities. It will come from the outside as Christ brings his Spirit into our life, and we give our life away to him in fundamental and consistent ways. It is possible to be a fundamentally and consistently happy person in this world. Not by our own power or by our might but by the Spirit of God, for "with man it is impossible, but not with God. For all things are possible with God" (Mark 10:27).

Paul wrote, "Do all things without grumbling or disputing, that you may be blameless and innocent, children of God without blemish in the midst of a crooked and twisted generation, among whom you shine as lights in the world, holding fast to the word of life" (Philippians 2:14-16). Do all things without grumbling. Be cheerful. Be the happy church. And what happens? We shine like lights in the midst of a darkened world.

Maybe now we see why C. S. Lewis says it is a "duty" to be happy. Why something like the mood or tone or culture of our church is so important. Feelings are dismissed as superficial and the pursuit of happiness as a shallow act, but we have had enough of being taught to be dour-faced, dutiful workers for Christ when Christ has called us to *joyful* obedience.

It *is* our duty—the duty of the church—to be the happy people of God. When we fight for this happiness, live into the joy won for us by Jesus Christ, the happy people of God shine in this world. The happy church once again will be a lighthouse in the dark night, a beacon in the fog.

I once met the pastor of a very active church in Welch, West Virginia, the seat of one of the poorest counties in America. The church was thriving. I asked him what they were doing right. He said, "Tim, when they called me to this church to be the pastor, I wasn't sure I wanted to do it. I gathered the elders and told them, 'I grew up in this town. When I was a boy, I got run out of all those grumpy churches downtown who didn't want dirty coal-miners' kids messing up their carpets and velour pews. Well, those grumpy churches are all empty now. I'll be the pastor here, but it's going to be different. It's going to be noisy, it's going to be messy, and there's going to be a lot of kids!'"

I looked around. It was noisy. It was messy. There were a lot of kids. And they were happy!

Sometimes it simply takes a leader to say, "You know, we are allowed to be happy." The mission God has given us is beautiful. The gifts God has given us are beautiful. Your church has exactly what it needs to follow Christ in faithfulness and to know his joy.

What does a happy church do? It reads the Bible to build up one another in love. It sings with passion and prays openly with divine intimacy. The happy church loves laughter, knowing it is a symbol of Christ's victory. It hopes without limits and dreams big dreams before God. The happy church takes on the mission to spread gladness to the suffering, knowing God's joy is greater than the world's sadness. The happy church shares its meals as foretaste of the kingdom—it knows where it is headed.

> **Your church has exactly what it needs to follow Christ in faithfulness and to know his joy.**

Your church already does all these things. I know it does. There's no program to buy, no subscription service or mail-order kit. God has already given you the foundations for happiness. It's an every-member exercise. You can be a leader in your church's happiness.

Bring a smile. Share a laugh. Offer a prayer. Where happiness has dried up, pray for the grace of God to pour down once again and restore it. Resolve today to stand for joy in your community of faith. God has done so much for you.

So, be the happy church. Be the happy church because God has laid the foundations and bulwarks of your happiness. Be the happy church because God enjoys your enjoyment of him. Be the happy church as a witness to the glory of God and the victories of Christ. Be the happy church because the broken world needs an embodiment of the wholeness and joy found only in Jesus. Be the happy church in a darkened world.

> Be glad in the LORD, and rejoice, O righteous,
>   and shout for joy, all you upright in heart! (Psalm 32:11)

> Shout for joy in the LORD, O you righteous!
>   Praise befits the upright. (Psalm 33:1)

Happiness is fitting for you who have been saved by Jesus. Praise befits the people of God. Joy suits your composition, gladness fits your gatherings, and happiness is your proper uniform. Put it on, won't you?

The happy church. It is God's gift to the redeemed and a signpost to heaven. It is yours to receive. Enjoy it.

Acknowledgments

My thanks pour out to the elders of my church for allowing me to devote time to putting these thoughts together. Many generous readers helped me to say things better including my friends Eddie Capparucci, Bob Gilbert, Tom Goodrich, Andrew Alden and Walter Henegar. I am grateful too for timely encouragement from John Ortberg and Glenn Lucke convincing me to keep at it. I can't express what a joy it has been to be adopted into the Inter-Varsity Press family. Many thanks to Don Everts for introducing me to this team and to Helen Lee for her sharp insights and generous enthusiasm. This book would still be a loose pile of notes if not for the remarkable talents of my wife, Abigail, who fed every page with insights. This book is dedicated to her, to the glory of God, who has brought us joy and happiness together.

Small Group
Discussion Questions

Chapter One: Getting Serious About Happiness

1. Think of a moment this month when you were genuinely happy. What made you happy? Is that a foundation for happiness you could return to again and again with the same result?

2. Do you think it is right for a Christian to expect happiness? Why or why not?

3. Are there activities or thoughts that produce happiness in you? Name them.

4. Do you think your friends and neighbors consider you a happy person? Do they connect that happiness to your faith in Christ?

5. How are people pursuing happiness in our times? How can a Christ-follower help them in their hope to be happy?

Exercise: Smile. We often allow our face to express our own inner feelings, whatever they may be at the moment. Use the expression on your face to communicate what God has done for you. Think about using your expression to communicate God's love to another as you enter church this week.

Chapter Two: Where Is the Happy Church?

1. Where do people most often gather to be happy and celebrate? Why these places and not others?

2. What is the happiest place or group of people you visit on a regular basis? Do you see your church as a community pursuing happiness together? If not, what is your church pursuing instead?

3. Which do you think makes a bigger impact outside the walls of the church: what a church believes or how a church acts?

4. Does your church matter to its community? What would be missing if your church suddenly disappeared?

5. Does the average person in our culture pursue happiness? How should the church serve that person?

Exercise: Bring a gift. Prepare yourself for church this week by coming with a gift. Not your money but a happy story, a joke or a meaningful event you could share with someone quickly on Sunday morning. Come with a gift and pray for the opportunity to share it.

Chapter Three: Satisfied in the Word

1. Do you think of the Bible as food? Is there a regular way that you take in and receive the Word of God as nourishment (daily reading, weekly study, etc.)?

2. How does your church think about the Bible? Is it a source of gladness? Give an example.

3. How would a non-Christian, or someone in your community who is not part of a church, describe the role of the Bible in the church? What do they think we think about the Bible?

4. Does the relationship a church has with the Bible change the way that church is viewed in the community? Can it open or close people's minds to the good news of Jesus Christ? How?

Exercise: Study. Take the Scripture from the weekly sermon and study it at home. If you know the passage for the next week, study it prior to coming to church. Your pastor will not be able to teach you all there is to know about a given passage! Go deeper with your own study of the Bible before and after the sermon.

Chapter Four: God's Instrument of Praise

1. What is your favorite thing to sing? Can you remember the first song you ever memorized all the way through? If so, name it.

2. Why do you think the church has so much singing in worship? Does it move you emotionally to sing at church? Why do you think God wants the church to sing?

3. Psalm 40:3 says, "He put a new song in my mouth, / a song of praise to our God." Why do you think the Scriptures celebrate the "new song"? Do you prefer a new song or an old song? Why? Is it okay to sing some old songs too? Why?

4. What is the happiest song you have ever heard?

5. How are the church's songs different from the world's songs? What topics do popular musicians sing about in our times? What do Christians sing about?

Exercise: Sing. Are you shy about singing praise? Practice. Sing in the car and in the shower, but when you get to church, do your best to sing with joy. Pay attention to the praise songs and learn them. Come early and look at the hymns in the hymnal prior to the service. Help the church to lift a song of praise.

Chapter Five: Prayers of the People

1. Do you pray regularly? What has been the most meaningful time or season of prayer for you? Who taught you how to pray?

2. How would you describe the prayer life of your church? What does the church pray for during worship? Are you quick to pray together? Why or why not?

3. How do outsiders describe the prayers of the church? If you were not a Christian, why would you say people in church pray? What would you say they are praying for, and why?

4. Have you prayed recently, simply to know God and know the joy of his constant presence? Do you think that prayer would make a difference in your life? Why?

5. What is your church praying for God to do in your midst?

Exercise: Small group prayer. Do you have a group small enough and regular enough that you know them and they know you? If not, you need one. Get into a small group. In that group, offer to pray this week. If you have never prayed aloud before, find a few verses of a psalm and offer to pray that for the group. Listen to the needs of the congregation, listen to the prayer requests of your friends and small group, and offer them to the Lord in prayer.

Chapter Six: Laughing Matters

1. Do you have a favorite moment in a movie or novel when laughter broke out and changed everything? How about in your own life? Explain.

2. What makes you laugh?

3. Is there much laughter in your church? Who leads the way in laughter? Is it contagious?

4. Do you find it easy or difficult to laugh or to be glad and cheerful? Why? Do you believe there is a duty to be cheerful at church? Why or why not?

5. In what ways do Christians take themselves too seriously? How do you think the world sees Christians, as cheerful or dour?

Exercise: Laugh out loud. Bring merriment to your church. Allow yourself to laugh. Allow someone to see you laugh. Don't get back in your car and head home from church this week until you've laughed out loud in the community of faith!

Chapter Seven: The People of Limitless Hope

1. Are you naturally optimistic? If so, do you always feel firm foundations for your optimism or do you sometimes fake it? Explain.

2. What are some reasons for a Christian to have hope?

3. Do you think of your church as a hope community? Do you feel more or less hopeful after a morning at your church? What feeds your hope at church, or what could nourish it better?

4. How could the church better share its hope with the world around it?

Exercise: Attend a memorial service. Why does it always seem unexpected when someone in the church dies? The most mature Christian disciples I know seem to turn up at almost every memorial service of our church. Consider it an act of Christian discipleship to attend the memorial service when a church member passes away; worship God and bear witness to the power of the resurrection. Pay attention to the prayers and to the Scriptures.

Chapter Eight: Suffering the Mission of Joy

1. Suffering is very personal and hard to talk about. Is there a time in your life when you felt the presence of God in suffering; when you felt God carrying you because you could not make it alone? If so, please describe it.

2. Is your church involved with the suffering found in its community? Are you?

3. Does your church grieve well? First Corinthians 12:26 says, "If one member suffers, all suffer together; if one member is honored, all rejoice together." Is this true of your church? Explain.

4. How does the world handle suffering? How do people get through hard times without Jesus or the church?

5. What should non-Christians see when they watch a Christian suffer? What should they see the church doing when a member suffers?

Exercise: Go on mission. Take up a mission opportunity in your church. Maybe there is a one-time opportunity to try (for example, making sandwiches for a local food ministry or taking collected resources to a local outreach). Maybe your church takes a trip every year or every quarter. Go on mission with your church. Move out to where there is pain, and see if the Lord brings relief to others through you.

Chapter Nine: The Future Feast We Taste

1. What are your favorite church celebrations?

2. How do you "taste and see" the goodness of God? What gets you in touch with God's joy?

3. Do you participate in meals at your church? If not, why? If so, what are they like? Do they have a spirit of celebration about them? Explain.

4. The parties we share now are a foretaste of the party in chapters 7 and 19 of Revelation. In that party, every nation, every people, every language will be represented. How can we try to enact that future reality now?

5. How does the world party? Are church parties different from worldly parties? How? Do non-Christians you know think highly of church parties? Why or why not?

Exercise: Make a pie. Make a pie and give it to your pastor! Just kidding. The next time there is an opportunity to share a meal at your church, prepare something or add something or serve something. See that meal as a foretaste of the kingdom. Invite someone you wouldn't ordinarily invite.

Chapter Ten: When the Church Is Heaven's Sunlight

1. Is the challenge to be happy at church easy or hard for you? Why? Have you ever considered it a duty or obligation to be cheerful at church? How does that strike you?

2. Are there people who challenge your ability to stay joyful? Why? How do you handle the pockets of discontent around you?

3. At what point should church leadership intervene with a consistently divisive or toxically discontented person in the church? How should that be handled?

4. Do you think your community sees your church as a culturally happy place? Why or why not?

5. If someone said, "I'm looking for more happiness in my life," would you invite them to your church?

Exercise: Be good news. How can you help your church be good news to your community? Hold a prayer vigil and go door-to-door asking, How can we pray for you? Challenge your small group to find a way to bless the neighborhood where you meet. Pray for the health of your church and work to maintain it. The greatest gift you can give your community is a healthy and happy church.

Notes

Foreword

[1]Jonathan Edwards, "The End for Which God Created the World," in John Piper, *God's Passion for His Glory* (Wheaton, IL: Crossway, 1998), 244.

Chapter One: Getting Serious About Happiness

[1]C. S. Lewis, *Letters to Malcolm: Chiefly on Prayer* (New York: Mariner Books, 1992), 93.

[2]John Ortberg, *Soul Keeping: Caring for the Most Important Part of You* (Grand Rapids: Zondervan, 2014), 48.

[3]Psalms 1; 2; 32; 33; 34; 40; 41; 65; 84; 89; 94; 106; 112; 119; 127; 128; 144; 146 with *asher*, and Psalms 5; 16; 30; 32; 34; 35; 43; 86; 90; 92; 97; 105; 113; 122; 126; 137 with a synonym. See Ellen Charry, *God and the Art of Happiness* (Grand Rapids: Eerdmans, 2010), 199.

[4]Frederick Dale Bruner, *Matthew: A Commentary* (Grand Rapids: Eerdmans, 2004), 1:159.

Chapter Two: Where Is the Happy Church?

[1]Simon Sinek, *Start with Why* (New York: Penguin, 2011), 129.

[2]Billy Graham, "Be Not Anxious," Billy Graham Evangelistic Association, accessed July 13, 2015, http://billygraham.org/devotion/be-not-anxious.

[3]Westminster Larger Catechism, Q. 135.

[4]C. S. Lewis, quoted in Sheldon Vanauken, *A Severe Mercy* (New York: Harper & Row, 1977), 189.

[5]C. S. Lewis, "Sometimes Fairy Stories May Say Best What's to Be Said," *New York Times*, November 18, 1956, http://apilgriminnarnia.com/2014/01/27/sometimes-fairy-stories.

[6]Eugene Peterson, *A Long Obedience in the Same Direction* (Downers Grove, IL: InterVarsity Press, 2000), 54.

[7]See 1 Peter 2:9; Ephesians 1:13-14; 1 Thessalonians 5:9; Romans 5:8-10; Ephesians 2:4-5; Romans 8:1; Romans 5:1; 1 Peter 1:3-5; Romans 6:23; Psalm 119:105; Isaiah 9:2; Psalm 1:3.

[8]Blaise Pascal, *Pascal's Pensées* 425, trans. W. F. Trotter (New York: E. P. Dutton, 1958), 113, quoted in John Piper, *Desiring God* (Colorado Springs: Multnomah, 2003), 19.

[9]Aristotle, *Nicomachean Ethics* 1.5, in *Aristotle On Man in the Universe*, ed. Louise Ropes Loomis (New York: Gramercy, 1943), 91.

[10]Augustine, *The Confessions*, trans. Maria Boulding (New York: New City Press, 1997), 14.

[11]Augustine, *Confessions*, trans. R. S. Pine-Coffin (London: Penguin, 1961), 40.

[12]Dallas Willard, *Renovation of the Heart: Putting On the Character of Christ* (Colorado Springs: NavPress, 2012), 68.

[13]Ellen Charry, *God and the Art of Happiness* (Grand Rapids: Eerdmans, 2010), xi.

[14]Piper, *Desiring God*, 286.

[15]Augustine, *Enchiridion on Faith, Hope, and Love*, trans. J. B. Shaw (Washington, DC: Regnery, 1996), 18.

Chapter Three: Satisfied in the Word

[1]Justin Martyr, *First Apology*, Ancient Christian Writers 56, trans. L. W. Barnard (New York: Paulist Press, 1997), 71.

[2]Martin Luther, "Freedom of a Christian," in *Martin Luther: Three Treatises* (Philadelphia: Fortress Press, 1970), 279.

[3]Martin Luther, *Luther's Works, Sermons 1*, vol. 51, ed. John W. Doberstein and Helmut T. Lehmann (Philadelphia: Fortress Press, 1966), 77.

[4]Westminster Confession 1.2, 1.5.

[5]Laugh Out Loud, Talk to You Later, What Are You Doing? Be Right Back, For What It's Worth, Rolling on the Floor Laughing.

[6]Robert L. Wilken, "Introducing the Athanasian Creed," *Currents in Theology and Mission*, February 1979, 9.

[7]Henry Cloud, *Boundaries for Leaders* (New York: HarperCollins, 2013), 28.

[8]Dallas Willard, *Renovation of the Heart: Putting on the Character of Christ* (Colorado Springs: NavPress, 2012), 95.

[9]John Stott, *You Can Trust the Bible* (Grand Rapids: Discovery House, 1991), 18.

[10]Westminster Larger Catechism, Q. 157.

Chapter Four: God's Instrument of Praise

[1]Karl Barth, *Church Dogmatics* 4.3.2, trans. George W. Bromiley (Edinburgh: T&T Clark, 1962), 866.

[2]Ibid., 867.

[3]Hughes Oliphant Old, *Worship: Reformed According to Scripture* (Louisville, KY: Westminster John Knox Press, 2002), 33.

[4]Athanasius, *Letter to Marcellinus*, in *Athanasius: The Life of Antony and the Letter to Marcellinus*, trans. Robert C. Gregg (New York: Paulist Press, 1980), 124.

[5]Ibid., 125-26.

[6]John Ortberg, *Soul Keeping: Caring for the Most Important Part of You* (Grand Rapids: Zondervan, 2014), 170.

[7]Ann Voskamp, *One Thousand Gifts* (Grand Rapids: Zondervan, 2010), 176.

[8]Old, *Worship*, 42.

[9]Andy Crouch, *Culture Making: Recovering Our Creative Calling* (Downers Grove, IL: InterVarsity Press, 2008), 77.

[10]Thomas Ken, "Awake, My Soul, and with the Sun," 1674.

[11]Old, *Worship*, 37.

[12]Anicius Manlius Severinus Boethius, *The Consolation of Philosophy* 3.9.23, quoted in Ellen Charry, *God and the Art of Happiness* (Grand Rapids: Eerdmans, 2010), 77.

[13]Anicius Manlius Severinus Boethius, "The Bent of Nature," in *The Consolation of Philosophy of Boethius*, trans. H. R. James (London: Elliot Stock, 1897), 99.

[14]Augustine, *Confessions*, trans. R. S. Pine-Coffin (London: Penguin, 1961), 190.

Chapter Five: Prayers of the People

[1]Dietrich Bonhoeffer, *Life Together*, Dietrich Bonhoeffer Works 5 (Minneapolis: Fortress Press, 1996), 69.

[2]W. Bingham Hunter, "The Prayer-Obedience Relationship," *Knowing & Doing Journal*, Winter 2008, 1.

[3]Clement of Alexandria, *Stromateis* 7.

[4]Richard Foster, *Prayer: Finding the Heart's True Home* (San Francisco: HarperCollins, 2002), 22.

[5]Ibid.

[6]John Stott, *Romans: God's Good News for the World* (Downers Grove, IL: InterVarsity Press, 1994), 389.

[7]Richard Foster, *Celebration of Discipline*, rev. ed. (San Francisco: Harper-Collins, 1978), 33.

[8]John Calvin, *Institutes of the Christian Religion* 3.20.1, trans. F. L. Battles (Philadelphia: Westminster Press, 1960), 850.

[9]Thom S. Rainer, *Autopsy of a Deceased Church: 12 Ways to Keep Yours Alive* (Nashville: B&H Publishers, 2014), chap. 9.

[10]Mark Batterson, *All In* (Grand Rapids: Zondervan, 2013), 87.

[11]Charles Haddon Spurgeon, *The C. H. Spurgeon Collection* (Albany, OR: Ages Software, 1999), 1.120.

[12]Bonhoeffer, *Life Together*, 57.

[13]Dietrich Bonhoeffer, *Letters and Papers from Prison* (New York: Touchstone, 1997), 419.

Chapter Six: Laughing Matters

[1]Charles Haddon Spurgeon, *The C. H. Spurgeon Collection* (Albany, OR: Ages Software, 1999), 1:97.

[2]Ignatius of Antioch, *To the Ephesians* 9, trans. Bart Ehrman, in *The Apostolic Fathers*, Loeb Classical Library 24 (Cambridge, MA: Harvard University Press, 2003), 1:229.

[3]Ellen Charry, *God and the Art of Happiness* (Grand Rapids: Eerdmans, 2010), 250.

[4]Marshall Brain, "How Laughter Works," *How Stuff Works*, accessed July 20, 2015, http://science.howstuffworks.com/life/laughter1.htm.

[5]Ibid.

[6]Eugene Peterson, *A Long Obedience in the Same Direction* (Downers Grove, IL: InterVarsity Press, 2000), 100-101.

[7]C. S. Lewis, *Screwtape Letters* (New York: Touchstone, 1996), 83.

[8]Charles Dickens, quoted in Thomas W. Hanford, *2010 Popular Quotations* (Albany, OR: Ages Software, 1997), 303.

[9]Richard Foster, *The Celebration of Discipline*, rev. ed. (San Francisco: Harper-Collins, 1978), 197.

[10]G. K. Chesterton, *Orthodoxy* (Wheaton, IL: Harold Shaw, 1994), 114.

[11]Søren Kierkegaard, *Fear and Trembling*, trans. Howard Hong and Edna Hong (Princeton, NJ: Princeton University Press, 1983), 41.

[12]Chesterton, *Orthodoxy*, 172. This is the closing line of the book.

Chapter Seven: The People of Limitless Hope

[1]Ellen Charry, *God and the Art of Happiness* (Grand Rapids: Eerdmans, 2010), 167.

[2]Richard Hays, *First Corinthians*, Interpretation Commentary (Louisville, KY: John Knox Press, 1997), 260.

[3]Kevin DeYoung, *The Good News We Almost Forgot* (Chicago: Moody Publishers, 2010), 41.

[4]This is based on a similar illustration by Tim Keller in "Search for Happiness," a sermon delivered at Redeemer Presbyterian Church, New York City, September 12, 1993.

[5]C. S. Lewis, *Mere Christianity* (New York: Macmillan, 1952), 104.

[6]Ann Voskamp, *One Thousand Gifts* (Grand Rapids: Zondervan, 2010), 176.

[7]Isabel Best, ed., *The Collected Sermons of Dietrich Bonhoeffer* (Minneapolis: Fortress Press, 2012), 208.

[8]Dietrich Bonhoeffer, *Letters and Papers from Prison* (New York: Touchstone, 1997), 419.

[9]Steve Hayner and Sharol Hayner, *Joy in the Journey: Finding Abundance in the Shadow of Death* (Downers Grove, IL: InterVarsity Press, 2015), 32-33.

[10]Edward Mote, "My Hope Is Built on Nothing Less," 1834.

[11]Steven Vryhof, "Crash Helmets and Church Bells," *Perspectives*, August-September 2000, 3.

Chapter Eight: Suffering the Mission of Joy

[1]Augustine, *The City of God Against the Pagans*, trans. R. W. Dyson (Cambridge: Cambridge University Press, 1998), 924.

[2]John Piper, *Desiring God* (Colorado Springs: Multnomah, 2003), 286.

[3]Hannah Whitall Smith, *The Christian's Secret of a Happy Life*, in *Devotional Classics*, ed. Richard Foster and James Bryan Smith (San Francisco: Harper-Collins, 1993), 265.

[4]Barbara Fredrickson, Steven Cole et al., "A Functional Genomic Perspective on Human Well-Being," *Proceedings of the National Academy of the Sciences* 110, no. 33 (2013): 13684-689.

[5]Don Everts, *Go and Do: Becoming a Missional Christian* (Downers Grove, IL: InterVarsity Press, 2012), 128.

[6]Bill Hybels, *Courageous Leadership* (Grand Rapids: Zondervan, 2009), 23.

[7]Ellen Charry, interviewed by Ken Myers, *Mars Hill Audio Journal* 107, March 1, 2011.

[8]Charles Haddon Spurgeon, *The C. H. Spurgeon Collection* (Albany, OR: Ages Software, 1999), 1:97.

[9]John Ortberg, *Love Beyond Reason* (Grand Rapids: Zondervan, 1998), 26.

[10]John Ortberg, *Soul Keeping: Caring for the Most Important Part of You* (Grand Rapids: Zondervan, 2014), 180.

[11]Ibid., 184.

[12]C. S. Lewis, *The Lion, the Witch, and the Wardrobe* (New York: Collier, 1970), 159.

Chatper Nine: The Future Feast We Taste

[1]Jonathan Edwards, "A Divine and Supernatural Light Immediately Imparted to the Soul," in *The Works of Jonathan Edwards* (Peabody, MA: Hendrickson, 1998), 2:14.

[2]Origen of Alexandria, *Contra Celsum*, trans. Henry Chadwick (Cambridge: Cambridge University Press, 1953), 44.

[3]From the original Greek. See J. N. D. Kelly, *Early Christian Creeds*, 3rd ed. (London: Continuum, 1972), 298.

[4]"But the Holy Spirit is the source of holiness." Basil of Caesarea, *Against Eunomius* 3.2, trans. Mark DelCogliano and Andrew Radde-Gallwitz (Washington, DC: Catholic University Press, 2011), 188.

[5]Charles Dickens, *A Christmas Carol* (Mahwah, NJ: Watermill Press, 1980), 44.

[6]Ibid., 48.

[7]John Nolland, *Luke 9:21-18:34*, Word Biblical Commentary 35b (Dallas: Word Books, 1993), 782.

[8]Kenneth E. Bailey, *The Cross and the Prodigal* (Downers Grove, IL: InterVarsity Press, 2005), 67.

[9]Tim Keller, *The Prodigal God* (New York: Penguin, 2008), 82-83.

[10]Ibid., 103.

Chapter Ten: When the Church Is Heaven's Sunlight

[1]Cyprian of Carthage, *Letter to Donatus*, in *Ante-Nicene Fathers*, ed. Alexander Roberts and James Donaldson (New York: Scribner's, 1903), 5:277.

[2]George Hodges, *Saints and Heroes to the End of the Middle Ages* (Chapel Hill, NC: Yesterday's Classics, 2006), 3.

[3]Robert Louis Wilken, *The First Thousand Years* (New Haven, CT: Yale University Press, 2012), 73.

[4]C. S. Lewis, *Mere Christianity* (New York: Macmillan, 1952), 105-6.

[5]Lesslie Newbigin, *The Gospel in a Pluralist Society* (Grand Rapids: Eerdmans, 1989), 234.

[6]Charles Haddon Spurgeon, *The C. H. Spurgeon Collection* (Albany, OR: Ages Software, 1999), 1:545.

[7]Tim Keller, "Search for Happiness," sermon delivered at Redeemer Presbyterian Church, New York City, September 12, 1993.